Mathematics Formative Assessment

Volume 2

50 More Practical Strategies for Linking Assessment, Instruction, and Learning

PAGE KEELEY

CHERYL ROSE TOBEY

A JOINT PUBLICATION

NATIONAL COUNCIL OF
TEACHERS OF MATHEMATICS

FOR INFORMATION:

Corwin

A SAGE Company

2455 Teller Road

Thousand Oaks, California 91320

(800) 233-9936

www.corwin.com

SAGE Publications Ltd.

1 Oliver's Yard

55 City Road

London EC1Y 1SP

United Kingdom

SAGE Publications India Pvt. Ltd.

B 1/I 1 Mohan Cooperative Industrial Area

Mathura Road, New Delhi 110 044

India

SAGE Publications Asia-Pacific Pte. Ltd.

3 Church Street

#10-04 Samsung Hub

Singapore 049483

Program Director: Jessica Allan

Senior Associate Editor: Kimberly Greenberg

Editorial Assistant: Katie Crilley

Production Editor: Melanie Birdsall

Copy Editor: Deanna Noga

Typesetter: C&M Digitals (P) Ltd.

Proofreader: Wendy Jo Dymond

Indexer: Molly Hall

Cover Designer: Karine Hovsepian

Marketing Manager: Margaret O'Connor
and Nicole Osborne

ISBN: 978-1-5063-1139-5
LCCN: 2011019158

This book is printed on acid-free paper.

17 18 19 20 21 10 9 8 7 6 5 4 3 2 1

Contents

Preface

HOW THIS BOOK FITS WITH
THE OTHER BOOKS IN THIS SERIES

In the last decade, a great many books have been published on formative assessment. These books, usually intended for a general audience, address the importance of formative assessment, the research that supports it, how it is used formally and informally, and they also include examples. Most of these books provide only a few mathematics examples and are seldom authored by mathematics or STEM (science, technology, engineering, and mathematics) specialists. When mathematics examples are included, they rarely contain conceptual examples of mathematics that reflect current mathematical thinking.

In 2008, the first edition of *Science Formative Assessment: 75 Practical Strategies for Linking Assessment, Instruction, and Learning* was published (Keeley, 2008). Finally, science teachers had a formative assessment resource they could use that was science specific and authored by an experienced and well-respected leader in science education. In 2011, the mathematics version of the science book, *Mathematics Formative Assessment: 75 Practical Strategies for Linking Assessment, Instruction, and Learning,* was published with coauthor and mathematics specialist, Cheryl Rose Tobey.

Instead of a one-size-fits-all generic approach across all subject areas, *Mathematics Formative Assessment: 75 Practical Strategies for Linking Assessment, Instruction, and Learning* was designed to specifically address formative assessment considerations in mathematics and include examples that reflect the nature of mathematics teaching and learning. This book provided 75 formative assessment classroom techniques, referred to by the acronym FACTs, which mathematics educators could use to elicit common, research-based misconceptions, misunderstandings, and common errors as well as feedback on student learning throughout a cycle of instruction. These 75 FACTs promote thinking and mirror practices used by mathematicians to make sense of the numerical world.

As assessments for learning, the 75 FACTs ultimately help teachers build a bridge between where students are to where they need to be in their mathematical understanding. These 75 FACTs have been used by thousands of K–12 teachers, university faculty, and professional developers, in the United States and internationally, to both inform and transform teaching and learning in mathematics.

A second science volume, *Science Formative Assessment: 50 More Practical Strategies for Linking Assessment, Instruction, and Learning*, authored by Page Keeley, was published in 2015. Many of the same FACTs that are included in the second volume of science FACTs are included in this new mathematics Volume 2 version. FACTs that were science-specific were replaced with mathematics-specific FACTs, as well as some new FACTs that can be used across disciplines. Twenty-five new FACTs were added, and 25 FACTs from the science Volume 2 were repeated with mathematics examples. Not counting the overlap in strategies, these four books in science and mathematics provide educators with a total collection of 163 FACTs. Now mathematics teachers have an extensive collection of 125 mathematics FACTs, and for teachers who teach multiple disciplines, there is now a combined collection of 163 FACTs that can be used across subjects.

PURPOSE AND NEED

Why so many formative assessment strategies teachers can use to inform their teaching and promote learning? Good teachers have a repertoire of purposeful and effective strategies they use to move students' learning forward, while at the same time understanding where their students are in their thinking at any point during a cycle of instruction. They do not use the same strategies over and over until students tire of them. Having a rich and robust repertoire of purposeful strategies brings variety to instruction and motivates and engages learners.

Having a full toolbox of strategies (FACTs) to pull from is not enough. Teachers need to know how, when, and for what purpose to use a FACT. They need to know what stage in an instructional cycle a FACT is best used. Should it be used for elicitation or to check whether students have grasped and can apply the concept or practice? Is it helpful in bringing misconceptions to the surface? Teachers need to know in what format the FACT should be used. Should it be used individually at first and then in a small-group format? Which FACTs work well in a whole-class discussion format? Teachers need to connect the FACT to a learning goal and think about how students will get feedback to know how they are moving toward the intended outcome of a lesson.

The description of each FACT provides information on how the FACT promotes learning, how it informs instruction, how it should be implemented, connections to standards, modifications for different types of learners, and caveats to be aware of when using the FACT. This information is specific to each FACT and will help teachers use the strategy effectively. However, it is important to take the time to gain a broader understanding of mathematics formative assessment in general and how it inextricably links instruction, assessment, and learning. For this reason, I strongly suggest you read Chapters 1 through 3 in *Mathematics Formative Assessment: 75 Practical Strategies for Linking Assessment, Instruction, and Learning* (Keeley & Tobey, 2011) as a companion to this book, because this important information is not repeated in this volume.

AUDIENCE

The primary audience for this book is K–12 teachers who teach mathematics and preservice teachers preparing to teach mathematics; however, many of the formative assessment techniques described in this book can be used in other disciplines besides mathematics. College instructors can also use the techniques in this book. Professional developers, instructional coaches, mentors, and anyone who works with teachers can benefit from using the formative assessment classroom techniques to design, facilitate, and monitor adult learning.

ORGANIZATION

Chapter 1 opens with a classroom snapshot and describes the important link between assessment and learning. It describes the big idea of formative assessment and breaks it down into five key strategies. The chapter further elaborates on two major ways to use the formative assessment techniques in mathematics—as an elicitation strategy and to support productive mathematics talk. It concludes with considerations for next steps and provides a table of all 163 FACTs in the four books in this series.

Chapter 2 describes the link to content and practices that are in most states' mathematics standards. Table 2.1 lists the grade-level examples included in Chapter 3 that illustrate how a FACT is used and the concept and key mathematical idea targeted by the example. Table 2.2 shows how mathematical practices are linked to the 50 FACTs in Chapter 3.

Chapter 3 is the heart of the book. It includes a collection of 50 FACTs. The FACTs are arranged in alphabetical order so they can be easily located by name. Each section uses a common format, with a brief description of the FACT, how the FACT promotes student learning, how it informs instruction, how to develop and use the FACT, a content specific example of using the FACT in mathematics, general attributes, links to Standards for Mathematical Practice, modifications for different types of learners, caveats to be aware of, uses in other disciplines besides mathematics, and a brief example of how it is used in another discipline. Space is provided at the end of each section for you to record notes on how you used the FACT and considerations for further use.

There is also an Appendix with an annotated list of resources that can be used with the FACTs, as well as resources to extend your learning.

Acknowledgments

Thank you to all the teachers and mathematics coordinators and specialists with whom we have had the pleasure to work, whether in building your capacity to effectively use mathematics formative assessment in your classroom or in your work with teachers. There are too many wonderful and exceptional colleagues to list here, but know that we are deeply indebted to you all for supporting our work and giving us the opportunity to make a difference in your teaching and in your students' learning. Thanks to you all for trying out these FACTs and providing us with feedback.

We gratefully acknowledge our Corwin editor, Jessica Allan, for her infinite patience, unwavering support, and gentle nudges to finish the book for teachers who are eagerly awaiting this book. We also want to thank the terrific staff at Corwin for the extraordinary support you provide your authors and your commitment to high quality professional development. We also want to thank NCTM (National Council for Teachers of Mathematics) for copublishing this book and being the national voice for mathematics teaching and learning.

About the Authors

Page Keeley is an author, speaker, and consultant who works with school districts and STEM organizations throughout the United States and internationally in the areas of formative assessment and teaching for conceptual change. She recently retired from the Maine Mathematics and Science Alliance (MMSA) where she was the Senior Science Program Director for 16 years, directing projects and developing resources in the areas of leadership, professional development, linking standards and research on learning, formative assessment, and mentoring and coaching. She has been Principal Investigator and Project Director of three National Science Foundation (NSF)–funded projects, including the Northern New England Co-Mentoring Network; PRISMS: Phenomena and Representations for Instruction of Science in Middle School; and Curriculum Topic Study: A Systematic Approach to Utilizing National Standards and Cognitive Research. In addition to NSF-funded projects, she has directed state Math-Science Partnership (MSP) projects, including TIES K–12: Teachers Integrating Engineering into Science K–12, and a National Semi-Conductor Foundation grant, Linking Science, Inquiry, and Language Literacy (L-SILL). Keeley also founded and directed the Maine Governor's Academy for Science and Mathematics Education Leadership, a replication of the National Academy for Science Education Leadership, of which she is a fellow.

Keeley is the author of 18 books and numerous journal articles and book chapters. She is also a coauthor for McGraw-Hill's elementary and middle school science programs. Keeley taught high school science for 2 years and middle school mathematics and science for 12 years before leaving the classroom in 1996. At that time she was an active teacher leader at the state and national level. She served two terms as president of the Maine Science Teachers Association and was the District II National Science Teachers Association (NSTA) director. In 2008, Keeley was elected the 63rd president of the NSTA. She received the Presidential Award for

Excellence in Secondary Science Teaching in 1992, the Milken National Distinguished Educator Award in 1993, and was named the AT&T Maine Governor's Fellow in 1994.

As a nationally known professional developer and speaker, she received the National Staff Development Council's (now Learning Forward) Susan Loucks-Horsley Award for Leadership in Science and Mathematics Professional Development in 2009, and the National Science Education Leadership Association's Outstanding Leadership in Science Education Award in 2013. She has been a science education delegation leader for the People to People Citizen Ambassador Professional Programs, leading the South Africa trip in 2009, the China trip in 2010, the India trip in 2012, the Cuba trip in 2014, and the Peru trip in 2015.

Prior to teaching, Keeley was a research assistant in immunogenetics at the Jackson Laboratory of Mammalian Genetics in Bar Harbor, Maine. She received her BS in Life Sciences from the University of New Hampshire and her master's in Science Education from the University of Maine. She can be followed on Twitter @CTSKeeley and can be contacted through her website at www.uncoveringstudentideas.org or through Corwin for information about the professional development she and her colleagues provide.

 **Cheryl Rose Tobey** is mathematics specialist for Maine's Department of Education where she supports best practices in learning and teaching mathematics. She has recently served as a senior mathematics associate at Education Development Center (EDC) in Massachusetts primarily in the areas of formative assessment and professional development. She was the project director for Formative Assessment in the Mathematics Classroom: Engaging Teachers and Students (FACETS) and a mathematics specialist for Differentiated Professional Development: Building Mathematics Knowledge for Teaching Struggling Students (DPD); both projects are funded by the National Science Foundation (NSF). She also was director of development for an Institute for Educational Science (IES) project, Eliciting Mathematics Misconceptions (EM2).

Prior to joining EDC, Tobey was the senior program director for mathematics at the Maine Mathematics and Science Alliance (MMSA), where she served as the co-principal investigator of the mathematics section of the NSF-funded Curriculum Topic Study, and principal investigator and project director of two Title IIA state Mathematics and Science Partnership projects. Prior to working on these projects, Tobey was the co-principal investigator and project director for MMSA's NSF-funded Local Systemic Change Initiative, Broadening Educational Access to Mathematics in Maine (BEAMM), and she was a fellow in Cohort 4 of the

National Academy for Science and Mathematics Education Leadership. She is the coauthor of eleven published Corwin books, including seven books in the *Uncovering Student Thinking* series (2006–2014), two *Mathematics Curriculum Topic Study* resources (2006, 2012), *Bringing Math Students Into the Formative Assessment Equation* (2015), and *Mathematics Formative Assessment: 75 Practical Strategies for Linking Assessment, Instruction and Learning* (2010). Before joining MMSA in 2001 to begin working with teachers, Tobey was a high school and middle school mathematics educator for 10 years. She received her BS in secondary mathematics education from the University of Maine at Farmington and her MEd from City University in Seattle. She currently lives in Maine with her husband and blended family of five children.

Chapter 1

An Introduction to 50 More Formative Assessment Classroom Techniques (FACTs)

CLASSROOM SNAPSHOT OF FORMATIVE ASSESSMENT IN PRACTICE

Sixth-grade students are learning to multiply and divide fractions and mixed numbers. As an exit ticket several days into the unit, they individually complete a *Slide Sort* in which they are asked to use estimation to determine whether the quotient of two numbers is less than or more than 1. The teacher collects the exit tickets and looks at the students' responses and explanations prior to planning. As she examines the students' reasoning, she notices many are relying on rounding or calculating rather than reasoning about the size of the numbers. She realizes she needs to give them experiences with visual models using a series of problems that allow students to see patterns (i.e., dividing a larger fraction by a smaller fraction, dividing a smaller fraction by a larger fraction, dividing two fractions close in size). She creates the following *Learning Intention* and *Success Indicators* to focus students on what they will learn and how they will show they learned it.

Learning Intention: Reasoning about the size of fractions is helpful in determining estimates for the sum of two fractions

Success Indicator 1: I can use a strategy to determine whether a quotient is larger or smaller then a given benchmark.

Success Indicator 2: I can explain the strategies I use to estimate quotients of fractions and mixed numbers.

She then plans a series of scaffolded activities that provide opportunities for students to develop a conceptual meaning of division and reason about how the sizes of the dividend and divisor affect the size of the quotient, including building from whole numbers, thinking about division as how many __ are in __? (e.g., How many $\frac{1}{2}$ lbs are in 4 lbs?), and using models to find approximate and exact answers. Between activities, the teacher helps students *Take Stock* of their learning by revisiting the *Success Indicators*. During these discussions, she uses *Talk Moves* to probe further and assess students' understanding of various strategies for estimating the size of the quotient, being sure to include questions for different sizes of dividends and divisors. For example, after investigating the results of dividing a smaller number by a larger number, a student claims that when dividing a smaller number by a larger number the quotient will always be less than 1. After asking students to restate and support the claim in pairs and having several pairs share with the full group, she moves on to the next activity in the lesson.

The teacher concludes the lesson by referring students to the *Learning Intention* that was posted at the start of the lesson: "Reasoning about the size of fractions is helpful in determining estimates for the sum of two fractions." She uses the *Thumbs Up, Down, and Sideways* technique— a self-assessment for students to indicate the extent to which they feel they've met the three *Success Indicators* listed at the beginning of the lesson—as evidence of meeting the *Learning Intention* and then has the students do a quick write on *Success Indicator* 2 by asking students to explain at least two strategies for estimating the quotient of two fractions.

This brief classroom snapshot is an example of the inextricable link between formative assessment, good instruction, and learning. Formative assessment is frequently referred to as assessment *for* learning rather than assessment *of* learning, which is summative assessment. The preposition makes a difference as formative assessment's primary purpose is to inform instructional decisions and simultaneously support learning through continuous feedback to the learner. However, a third preposition can also be added: assessment *as* learning. You can see from the snapshot provided that purposeful formative assessment classroom techniques (FACTs) can become learning opportunities.

The FACTs described in this snapshot are just a few of the ways teachers can utilize various strategies to elicit students' ideas, monitor changes in their thinking, provide feedback, engage students in self-monitoring, and support reflection on learning. Throughout the process, the teacher is taking into account how well students are moving toward a learning target and what needs to be done to bridge the gap between where students are in their understanding and where they need to be. The 50 FACTs in this book, combined with the 75 FACTs in Volume 1 (Keeley & Tobey, 2011) will help you build an extensive repertoire of strategies that will inform instruction and promote learning—through a process called formative assessment. While you may be tempted to skip ahead and go directly to Chapter 3 to choose FACTs you can use in your classroom, you are encouraged to read the rest of this chapter and Chapter 2 so you can make effective use of the FACTs and strengthen your knowledge of formative assessment in mathematics instruction.

WHY 50 MORE FACTs?

Formative assessment is a process that informs instruction and supports learning, with instructional decisions made by the teacher or learning decisions made by the students being at the heart of the process. Dylan Wiliam (2011) describes the central idea of formative assessment as follows: "Evidence about learning is used to adjust instruction to better meet students needs—in other words, teaching is *adaptive* to the learner's needs" (p. 46). This overarching idea is broken down into five key strategies (Leahy, Lyon, Thompson, & Wiliam, 2005):

1. *Learning Intentions* and *Success Criteria*

2. Designing and facilitating productive classroom discussions, activities, and tasks that elicit evidence of learning

3. Providing feedback that moves learning forward

4. Activating learners as instructional resources for one another

5. Activating learners as the owners of their own learning

This book includes 50 new techniques that will help teachers and students utilize these five key strategies. In addition to the 75 FACTs published in the first volume of this series (Keeley & Tobey, 2011) and several of the FACTs in the science versions (Keeley, 2015, 2016) that are not repeated in the mathematics versions, teachers and teacher educators now have a total of 163 FACTs to embed throughout a cycle of instruction. Table 1.1 at the end of this chapter lists the combined collection of FACTs across all the current books in this series. A rich repertoire of FACTs helps learners interact with assessment in a variety of ways—writing, drawing, speaking, listening, questioning, investigating, modeling, and more.

Furthermore, these FACTs provide mathematics-specific examples that are often lacking in general formative assessment resources.

Misunderstandings are likely to develop as a normal part of learning mathematics. These misunderstandings can be classified as conceptual misunderstandings, overgeneralizations, preconceptions, partial conceptions, and common errors. Misconceptions are a problem in mathematics for two reasons. First, when students use them to interpret or apply them to new mathematics experiences, misconceptions interfere with their learning. Second, because students have often actively constructed their misconceptions, they are emotionally and intellectually attached to them. Even when students recognize that a misconception affects their learning, they are reluctant to let go of it (Tobey & Arline, 2014a, 2014b). For this reason it is important for teachers to have an expansive repertoire of effective techniques, such as the ones provided in this book, for uncovering, monitoring, and providing feedback on student thinking.

Another feature of the 50 new FACTs included in this book that is important in navigating today's mathematics education landscape is the connections to mathematics standards that include mathematics content, processes, and practices. Whether your state has its own mathematics standards or whether your state adopted the Common Core, the connection between the formative assessment classroom technique (FACT) and mathematics standards is included for each FACT.

The first volume of this book, *Mathematics Formative Assessment: 75 Practical Strategies for Linking Assessment, Instruction, and Learning* (Keeley & Tobey, 2011) includes important background information on formative assessment in mathematics. You are encouraged to obtain a copy of the first book as a companion to this volume to read and learn more about the following:

- Types of assessment and purposes for using formative assessment
- The research that supports formative assessment
- Classroom environments that support formative assessment
- The connection between teaching and learning
- Making the shift to a formative assessment-centered classroom
- Integrating assessment and instruction
- Metacognition
- The MAIL (Mathematics Assessment, Instruction, and Learning) Cycle
- Suggestions for selecting FACTs
- Suggestions for Implementing FACTs
- Using data from FACTs

Two purposes of formative assessment that are emphasized in this collection of 50 FACTs are elicitation of student thinking related to the learning goal and supporting productive math discourse, both of which relate directly to two of the National Council of Teachers of Mathematics' (NCTM) eight mathematical practices (NCTM, 2014). Each of these purposes has special nuances in mathematics that often are not explicitly addressed in general formative assessment strategies. While there are other purposes for which the FACTs are used in this book, it is important to understand these two purposes, because these are central to assessment *for* learning in mathematics.

ELICITATION FACTs

"Effective teaching involves finding the mathematics in students' comments and actions, considering what students appear to know in light of the intended learning goals and progression, and determining how to give the best response and support to students on the basis of their current understandings" (NCTM, 2014, p. 56). Elicitation FACTS are techniques that can be used to bring this Principle to Action to life in the classroom by supporting teachers in eliciting ideas both prior to and during the instructional cycle. Many of the Elicitation FACTs in this book are designed to draw out students' existing ideas, especially those that use faulty mathematics reasoning, so that responsive action can be taken. For example, many students struggle with the concept of fractions and decimals. Often the difficulty lies in overgeneralizations from their work with whole numbers. Students learning to compare fractions often treat the numerator and denominators as separate whole numbers, incorrectly identifying the fraction with the larger number in the denominator as the larger fraction (i.e., incorrectly reasoning that $\frac{1}{8}$ is larger than $\frac{1}{6}$). When comparing decimals, students often overgeneralize the rule used when comparing whole numbers, "a number with more digits is larger" (i.e., incorrectly reasoning that 0.235 is larger than 0.43). This is why elicitation of preexisting ideas is an important part of mathematics formative assessment.

Examples of Elicitation FACTs in this book include but are not limited to *Conjecture Cards, Ranking Tasks,* and *Slide Sort*. Elicitation FACTs that target preexisting ideas are used at the beginning of a unit, cluster of lessons, or a single lesson, as well as mid-instruction, to provide an opportunity for students to surface their initial ideas and give the teacher a sense of students' thinking prior to instruction. They are used to challenge students' existing ideas or conceptual models, uncover common errors in terminology use or interpretation of representations, and expose faulty explanations of common or familiar mathematics concepts. As a formative assessment that informs instruction, it helps the teacher gauge initial student thinking, plan for enacting or modifying the lesson to follow, gauge progress midstream to determine a responsive action, or choose a new lesson that better addresses where students are in their mathematical understanding. Using a FACT for elicitation promotes learning by engaging students, stimulating further thinking, and setting the stage for the activities and/or discussion that will follow.

When an Elicitation FACT is selected, it should be designed so that every student can have an answer or opinion, regardless of whether they are correct. The intent of using an Elicitation FACT is that every student will have an opportunity to share their thinking either verbally or through writing. The data from Elicitation FACTs help the teacher set learning goals for activities designed to address students' ideas, as well as eliminate activities that may not be necessary if students demonstrate conceptual understanding.

Early in the school year as you enact formative assessment, some students may feel uncomfortable sharing their initial ideas in a whole-class setting. This will eventually change as you work to establish a classroom culture that makes it safe to discuss and evaluate peer ideas. Your goal should be to eventually move students toward public sharing and critique of their thinking. In the meantime, you might consider using an anonymous elicitation strategy such as *Fingers Under Chin* or *Extended Sticky Bars*. One way you can anonymously share students' thinking as they are writing their responses to a FACT is to say, "As I walked around the room, I noticed several of you wrote . . ."; or, after you have collected students' written responses to a FACT and scanned through them, you might say, "I noticed several of you think . . ."; or you might list students' ideas or solutions on a chart as an initial record of the class thinking without critique at this point. These anonymous techniques provide a way for students to see that not everyone has the right answer and that in a mathematics community, students often have alternative explanations and ways of thinking. The goal is to work toward a common, accepted understanding by considering the ideas of others and gaining new information that can be used to construct mathematical explanations. These Elicitation FACTs also show students that you, the teacher, value their ideas regardless of whether they are right or wrong. Eventually students transition toward publicly sharing their thinking because they experience a learning environment where it is safe and interesting to share different ideas and ways of thinking.

First and foremost, remember the goal of elicitation is to promote student thinking, mentally commit to an answer, and participate in discussions (either immediately after an elicitation question is posed and/or in follow-up discussions) that reveal students' existing ideas. The biggest challenge for teachers right after students respond to an Elicitation FACT or during follow-up elicitation discussions, is to refrain from giving the answer and/or passing judgment on students' thinking. Let students grapple with ideas while you guide them toward understanding and a consensus of the best ideas or solutions.

Provide an opportunity for students to talk in pairs or in small groups before facilitating a whole-class discussion following use of an Elicitation FACT. Circulate and listen as students discuss their ideas and defend their arguments. When pairs or small groups are talking, the teacher's role should be as a facilitator who draws out the students' ideas without indicating right or wrong answers. Once students are told or are cued about the best answer, their thinking and questioning may stop. You want your students to keep thinking and discover the explanation for themselves, while you are gathering evidence of conceptual understanding or misunderstanding.

SUPPORTING PRODUCTIVE MATHEMATICS DISCOURSE

"Effective mathematics teaching engages students in discourse to advance the mathematical learning of the whole class. Mathematical discourse includes the purposeful exchange of ideas through classroom discussion, as well as through other forms of verbal, visual, and written communication" (NCTM, 2014, p. 29). As students talk, teachers listen. A treasure trove of formative assessment data can be mined merely by carefully listening to students talk about their ideas and justify their thinking.

However, discourse alone is not enough to promote learning and inform instruction. Mathematics discourse, or math talk, must be productive math talk. Productive talk is carefully orchestrated by the teacher using discussion norms in which all students are held accountable for each other's and their own learning in a respectful, safe environment. Furthermore, students must have something interesting to talk about, and they must be engaged through a variety a formats and techniques the teacher purposely uses to facilitate discussion. Several of the FACTs in this book are designed to be used in various talk formats.

For example, after using an Elicitation FACT in a small-group discussion, you may invite the whole class to take part in a discussion to share and critique the various ideas held by students. As you chart or make a visual record of the class ideas, make sure all students have an opportunity to share any thinking that may differ from the ideas already listed so you have a complete record of the class thinking. If you noticed during pair or small-group talk any significant thinking that was not shared during the process of listing the class ideas, you might say something like, "I heard one group talking about . . ." and add that to the list. Using *Talk Moves* helps encourage discussion.

Once you have generated a list of class ideas, facilitate a discussion to critique ideas by engaging the students in argumentation. The goal of argumentation is to seek understanding by putting forth ideas and persuading others to agree with your thinking, supporting it with evidence and sound mathematical reasoning. Encourage students to support their arguments in favor of or in rebuttal of one of the ideas listed by sharing evidence from previous experience, class activities, use of manipulatives, data from mathematical investigations, information from valid sources, and logic. As they engage in discussion and critique of arguments, the class usually comes to a consensus that some ideas can be discarded, narrowing the list to "our best thinking so far." This also provides the teacher with insight into students' thinking and the extent to which the class is moving toward understanding the mathematics concept.

Sometimes the discussion helps the class come to an accepted common understanding of the best answer and of why it is considered the best answer. Other times, students may leave class with unresolved ideas, "hanging out in uncertainty" until the next class period, when the teacher provides an opportunity for them to reexamine their thinking, test ideas, or gather more information to resolve the differences in their thinking. Some FACTs, especially ones that involve probing questions, can be discussed and resolved in less than 45 minutes; others may take a few days of carefully designed lessons. The formative nature of the FACT allows the teacher to encourage discourse and evidence-based learning experiences that will help students reshape and refine their thinking, keeping them engaged in moving toward the learning target until they have acquired the evidence they need to develop a conceptual understanding. Examples of FACTs that are used in talk formats include, but are not limited to, *I Think–I Rethink, Four Corners Jigsaw, Lines of Agreement,* and *VDR (Vote, Discuss, Revote).*

The challenge for teachers in using talk formats for formative assessment is deciding what to do with the student ideas you uncover during the use of talk and argument FACTs. Listening to students provides a lot of formative assessment data. Once you have uncovered these ideas, you will need to decide which ideas need to be considered in planning your next moves in instruction. It helps to categorize the ideas into valid ideas, partially valid ideas, minor misunderstandings, and major misconceptions. As you distill students' ideas that emerge from mathematics talk, think about your next steps in moving them toward the learning target. You may need to do the following:

1. Elicit further evidence of preconceptions or other conceptual obstacles

2. Confront students with examples that will challenge their existing ideas

3. Address misunderstandings related to the language of mathematics and other technical vocabulary

4. Reteach something that was taught previously but in a different context

5. Provide scaffolds to support students' developing understandings

6. Identify students who can be resources for other students during the lessons that will follow

7. Revisit the *Learning Intentions* and *Success Indicators* and adjust accordingly, depending on where students are in their understanding

8. Provide opportunities for students to access new information they can use to refine, reshape, or further develop their ideas

Several excellent resources are available to help you learn more about productive mathematics talk and how to orchestrate mathematics discussions in your classroom. The Appendix contains resources, tools, and strategies for engaging students in productive talk. These will help you use the FACTs that involve students in sharing and defending their ideas in a variety of talk formats.

NEXT STEPS

Remember, learning is like crossing a bridge. The elicitation question surfaces where students are at the beginning of the bridge. The bridge is the connection between students' initial ideas and the mathematics understanding. The instructional opportunities you provide through talk as well as investigative experiences and problem solving will take them over the bridge, sometimes in leaps, sometimes in small steps. Eventually you want students to end up on the other side of the bridge, without being carried over the bridge by the teacher, although some students may need a helping hand to guide them. It is that moment when the student realizes he or she has crossed over the bridge on his or her own, leaving ideas that no longer work for him or her behind, that results in powerful conceptual learning! As you use the FACTs described in Chapter 3, think about how they can be used to help you construct that conceptual bridge. Examine the links to the mathematics practices provided in the next chapter, as many of you will be building new bridges between where your students are and where they need to be in order to address the mathematical practices expectations in the Common Core State Standards or your existing state standards.

As you try out the FACTs in Chapter 3, add them to your growing repertoire of purposeful formative assessment techniques. Table 1.1 combines all the FACTs across the four books that currently exist for a total of 163 techniques across mathematics and science or 125 mathematics techniques. Some of them are new, and several have been around for decades. Some are specific to mathematics, while others can be used across disciplines. Be purposeful in selecting a FACT—know why you should use it and what you will learn from using it. But start small! As Dylan Wiliam (2011), a leader in formative assessment, wisely points out when being presented with so many formative assessment techniques and choices, "too much choice can be paralyzing—and dangerous. When teachers try to change more than two or three things about their teaching at the same time, the typical result is that their teaching will deteriorate and they go back to doing what they did before" (p. 161). His advice is to choose one or two to try out in your classroom. If they seem to be effective, practice using them until they become second nature. If they do not seem to be effective, consider how you can modify them to fit your teaching style and the needs of your learners or ask other teachers who are using them for advice on how to make them work. Not all these combined 125 techniques in mathematics will work for all teachers, but we are confident that you will find a few that will truly work for you and transform your teaching and your students' learning.

Table 1.1	163 Science and Mathematics Formative Assessment Classroom Techniques (FACTs)

1. A&D Statements ⊙→

2. Agreement Circles ⊙→

3. Always, Sometimes, or Never True →।

4. Annotated Student Drawings ⊙

5. B-D-A (Before–During–After) Drawings ।

6. Card Sorts ⊙→

7. Claim Cards ।

8. CCC—Collaborative Clued Corrections ⊙→

9. Chain Notes ⊙

10. C-E-O-SE ।

11. Comments Only/Comment Coding →।★

12. Commit and Toss ⊙→

13. Comparison Overlap Probes ।

14. Concept Attainment Cards →।

15. Concept Card Mapping ⊙→

16. Concept Cartoons ⊙→

17. Concept Mix-Up Probes ।★

18. Confidence Level Assessment (CLA) ।★

19. Conjecture Cards ★

20. Cover-Up ★

21. Create the Problem →

22. Cross-Cutter Cards ।

23. CSI (Color–Symbol–Image) ।

24. Data Match ⊙

25. Diagnostic Collections ।

26. Directed Paraphrasing ⊙

27. Enhanced Multiple Choice ।★

28. Error Analysis ★

29. Every Graph Tells a Story →।

30. Everyday Mystery Stories ।

31. Example, Nonexample →।

32. Explanation Analysis ⊙

33. Extended Sticky Bars ।★

34. Eye Contact Partners ।★

35. Fact-First Questioning ⊙→

36. Familiar Phenomenon Probes ⊙

37. Feedback Check-Ins ★

38. Feedback Focused Group Class Discourse ★

39. Feedback Sandwich ★

40. Feedback to Feed-Forward/ Feed Up, Feedback, and Feed Forward →।

⊙ In *Science Formative Assessment, Volume 1: 75 Practical Strategies for Linking Assessment, Instruction, and Learning* (Keeley, 2008, 2015).

→ In *Mathematics Formative Assessment, Volume 1: 75 Practical Strategies for Linking Assessment, Instruction, and Learning* (Keeley & Tobey, 2011).

। In *Science Formative Assessment, Volume 2: 50 More Practical Strategies for Linking Assessment, Instruction, and Learning* (Keeley, 2015).

★ In this volume, *Mathematics Formative Assessment, Volume 2: 50 More Practical Strategies for Linking Assessment, Instruction, and Learning*.

(Continued)

Table 1.1   (Continued)

41. Find Someone Who ★

42. Fingers Under Chin I★

43. First Word–Last Word ⊙

44. Fishbowl Think-Aloud ⊙

45. Fist to Five ⊙→

46. Flip the Question ★

47. Focused Listing ⊙

48. Four Corners ⊙→

49. Four Corners Jigsaw I★

50. Frayer Model ⊙→

51. Friendly Talk Probes ⊙→

52. Gallery Walk I★

53. Give Me Five ⊙→

54. Group Frayer Model I★

55. Group Talk Feedback I★

56. Guided Reciprocal Peer Questioning ⊙

57. Homework Card Sort I★

58. Hot Seat Questioning →I

59. Human Scattergraph ⊙→

60. I Think–I Rethink I★

61. I Think–We Think ⊙

62. I Used to Think . . . But Now I Know . . . ⊙→

63. Informal Student Interviews ⊙

64. Interactive Whole-Class Card Sorting ★

65. Interest Scale ⊙

66. Is It Fair? →

67. Juicy Questions ⊙

68. Justified List ⊙→

69. Justified True or False Statements ⊙→

70. K-W-L Variations ⊙→

71. Learning Goals Inventory (LGI) ⊙→

72. Learning Intentions I★

73. Learning Intentions Reflection ★

74. Let's Keep Thinking I★

75. Lines of Agreement I★

76. Look Back ⊙→

77. Magnetic Statements I

78. Matching Cards →I

79. Mathematician's Ideas Comparison→

80. Missed Conception ⊙

⊙ In *Science Formative Assessment, Volume 1: 75 Practical Strategies for Linking Assessment, Instruction, and Learning* (Keeley, 2008, 2015).

→ In *Mathematics Formative Assessment, Volume 1: 75 Practical Strategies for Linking Assessment, Instruction, and Learning* (Keeley & Tobey, 2011).

I In *Science Formative Assessment, Volume 2: 50 More Practical Strategies for Linking Assessment, Instruction, and Learning* (Keeley, 2015).

★ In this volume, *Mathematics Formative Assessment, Volume 2: 50 More Practical Strategies for Linking Assessment, Instruction, and Learning.*

81. More A–More B Probes →|

82. Most and Least Sure About ★

83. Muddiest Point ⊙ →

84. No-Hands Questioning ⊙ →

85. Now Ask Me a Question ★

86. Odd One Out ⊙ →

87. Opposing Views Probes →|

88. Overgeneralization Probes →

89. Paint the Picture ⊙

90. Partner Strategy Rounds ★

91. Partner Speaks ⊙→

92. Pass the Question ⊙

93. Pass the Problem →

94. P-E-O (Predict, Explain, Observe) Probes ⊙→

95. Peer-to-Peer Focused Feedback →

96. A Picture Tells a Thousand Words ⊙→

97. Picture This |

98. Plus–Delta |★

99. PMI (Plus–Minus–Interesting) |★

100. POMS—Point of Most Significance ⊙→

101. Popsicle Stick Questioning ⊙→

102. Prefacing ⊙

103. PVF—Paired Verbal Fluency ⊙→

104. Question Generating ⊙→

105. Questioning Cue Cards ★

106. Ranking Tasks |★

107. RAQ (Revise, Add, Question) Feedback |★

108. Recognizing Exceptions ⊙

109. Reflect Aloud ★

110. Reflect Then Self-Assess ★

111. Reflective Toss |

112. Refutations ⊙

113. Representation Analysis ⊙

114. RERUN ⊙

115. Response Cards →

116. "Rules That Expire" Probes ★

117. Same A–Same B Probes →

118. Scientists' Ideas Comparison ⊙

119. Seeing Structure ★

120. Sequencing Cards ⊙→

121. Slide Sort |★

122. Sort Envelopes ★

⊙ In *Science Formative Assessment, Volume 1: 75 Practical Strategies for Linking Assessment, Instruction, and Learning* (Keeley, 2008, 2015).

→ In *Mathematics Formative Assessment, Volume 1: 75 Practical Strategies for Linking Assessment, Instruction, and Learning* (Keeley & Tobey, 2011).

| In *Science Formative Assessment, Volume 2: 50 More Practical Strategies for Linking Assessment, Instruction, and Learning* (Keeley, 2015).

★ In this volume, *Mathematics Formative Assessment, Volume 2: 50 More Practical Strategies for Linking Assessment, Instruction, and Learning*.

(Continued)

Table 1.1 (Continued)

123. Sticky Bars ⊙→

124. STIP—Scientific Terminology Inventory Probe ⊙

125. Strategy Harvest →

126. Strategy Probe →

127. Structures for Taking Action ★

128. Student Evaluation of Learning Gains ⊙→

129. Student Interviews →

130. Success Indicators I★

131. Success Indicator Problem Generating ★

132. Synectics ⊙

133. Take Stock ★

134. Talk Moves I★

135. TAR (Target, Analogy, Reflection) I

136. Terminology Inventory Probe (TIP) →

137. Ten-Two ⊙→

138. Think-Alouds→

139. Thinking Log ⊙→

140. Think–Pair–Share ⊙→

141. Thermometer Feedback ★

142. Thought Experiments ⊙→

143. Three-Minute Pause ⊙→

144. Three-Two-One ⊙→

145. Thumbs Up, Thumbs Down/ Thumbs Up, Down, and Sideways →I

146. Traffic Light Cards ⊙→

147. Traffic Light Cups ⊙→

148. Traffic Light Dots ⊙→

149. Traffic Light Sliders I★

150. Two-Minute Paper ⊙→

151. Two or Three Before Me ⊙→

152. Two Stars and a Wish ⊙→

153. Two-Thirds Testing ⊙→

154. Vernacular Probes I

155. Volleyball—Not Ping Pong! ⊙→

156. VDR (Vote, Discuss, Revote) I★

157. Wait Time Variations ⊙→

158. What Are You Doing and Why? ⊙→

159. What Did I Learn Today? I

160. What Stuck With You Today? ★

161. Whiteboarding ⊙→

162. Word Sort →I

163. X Marks the Spot ★

⊙ In *Science Formative Assessment, Volume 1: 75 Practical Strategies for Linking Assessment, Instruction, and Learning* (Keeley, 2008, 2015).

→ In *Mathematics Formative Assessment, Volume 1: 75 Practical Strategies for Linking Assessment, Instruction, and Learning* (Keeley & Tobey, 2011).

I In *Science Formative Assessment, Volume 2: 50 More Practical Strategies for Linking Assessment, Instruction, and Learning* (Keeley, 2015).

★ In this volume, *Mathematics Formative Assessment, Volume 2: 50 More Practical Strategies for Linking Assessment, Instruction, and Learning.*

Chapter 2

Formative Assessment and Standards

As of this writing, several states have revised their mathematics standards or are considering revising their current standards. Some states have adopted the Common Core State Standards for Mathematics (CCSSO, 2010) in their entirety and others have used them to create their own standards. Still other states that have not begun the revision process, often due to legislatively mandated timelines, are nonetheless urging educators to incorporate the mathematical practices into their instruction.

It is beyond the scope of this book to provide an introduction to current mathematics standards since so many states have their own set of standards. However, if you are interested in how the FACTs relate to common sets of standards such as the Common Core State Standards for Mathematics, you can read more about that in Chapter 3 of *Mathematics Formative Assessment: 75 Practical Strategies for Linking Assessment, Instruction, and Learning* (Keeley & Tobey, 2011). The descriptions of each FACT in this book generally describe how each FACT supports key mathematical ideas and practices that are common to most state standards.

FACTs AND KEY IDEAS IN MATHEMATICS

All the 50 FACTs in Chapter 3 can be used to formatively assess students' thinking related to a concept and key idea in mathematics content domains such as numbers and operations, algebra, geometry, measurement, data analysis, and statistics. Table 2.1 summarizes the examples used in Chapter 3 to show which concepts are used as examples and the content domains. For some FACTs there is more than one grade level or concept example provided. For example, multiple grade-level examples are provided for *Success Indicators*. However, it is important to understand that FACTs are not limited to the grade level provided in the example. They can be used across Grades K–12 as well as in undergraduate education and in teacher professional development. The FACTs are not limited to the content in the example. They can be used to address a variety of concepts in mathematics found in different content domains. The table is merely provided to help you see the various ways FACTs can be used with mathematics content across all grade levels and domains of mathematics. Regardless of the state standards you are held accountable to teach, the concepts and key mathematical ideas in the table are likely to be similar to those that make up your own state standards or district curriculum. Therefore, this table can be used to help you think about connecting FACTs to standards or learning goals regardless of which state, district, or school learning outcomes guide teaching and learning in your setting.

FACTs AND MATHEMATICS PRACTICES

Mathematical practice standards describe varieties of expertise that mathematics educators at all levels should seek to develop in their students. These practices rest on important "processes and proficiencies" that have long been important to mathematics education (CCSSO, 2010). Most states have adopted the Standards for Mathematical Practice in the Common Core or adapted them for their own standards. Each FACT in Chapter 3 can be linked to a mathematical practice by (1) providing an opportunity for students to use the practice to think through and share their ideas, (2) providing an assessment opportunity for teachers to determine the extent to which students can use a mathematical practice, and (3) providing an opportunity for students to receive feedback on their use of the mathematical practice. The mathematical practices described in this book are from the Common Core. Even though some states have not adopted the Common Core, mathematical practices similar to the ones from the Common Core can be found in most states' standards:

Practice 1: Make sense of problems and persevere in solving them.

Practice 2: Reason abstractly and quantitatively.

Practice 3: Construct viable arguments and critique the reasoning of others.

Practice 4: Model with mathematics.

Practice 5: Use appropriate tools strategically.

Practice 6: Attend to precision.

Practice 7: Look for and make use of structure.

Practice 8: Look for and express regularity in repeated reasoning.

Table 2.2 designates which mathematical practices are most central when using a FACT. For some FACTs, all the practices can be used with the FACT, depending on the teaching and learning purposes. For example, *Confidence Level Assessment* may be used with any of the mathematical practices, especially if the FACT is used to find out how confident students are in using the mathematical practice. For some FACTs there may be only one or two practices associated with the FACT. For example, *Traffic Light Sliders* are used for problem solving. As you use the FACTs you might determine other ways a FACT can be used with a mathematical practice that is not designated on Table 2.2. It all depends on your instructional and assessment purpose.

FACTs can provide a starting point for learning key ideas and practices in mathematics standards. They can be used to monitor students' progress toward achieving performance expectations laid out in the standards and to adjust instruction so that all students will have opportunities to meet performance expectations. FACTs can be used to provide feedback to students or engage them in providing feedback to others, which they can use to improve or revise their thinking, thus taking responsibility for their own learning. FACTs help them ascertain what they need to improve their ability to use mathematical key ideas and practices and provide metacognitive and reflective opportunities for students to examine their own thinking and recognize how their ideas have changed. The social interaction involved when students are engaged in using FACTs models what today's mathematics classroom should be like—a classroom rich in discourse and generating ideas. Now, let's get the FACTs and build a repertoire of strategies that will transform teaching and learning in your classroom.

Table 2.1 Examples of FACTs Linked to Mathematics Content

FACT and Figure	Grade-Level Example	Concept(s)	Mathematics Domain
1. Comment Coding	6–8	Data Analysis	Measurement and Data
2. Concept Mix-Up Probes Figure 3.1	6–8	Algebraic Expression	Expressions and Equations
3. Confidence Level Assessment (CLA) Figure 3.2	3–5	Array Model of Multiplication	Number and Operations in Base 10
4. Conjecture Cards Figures 3.3 and 3.4	6–8	Inequalities	Expressions and Equations
5. Cover-Up	6–8	Equivalent Fractions	Number and Operations—Fractions
6. Enhanced Multiple Choice Figure 3.5	3–5	Estimating Quotients	Number and Operations—Fractions
7. Error Analysis	3–5	Comparing Fractions	Number and Operations—Fractions
8. Extended Sticky Bars Figures 3.6, 3.7, 3.8, and 3.9	9–12	Linear Equations	Algebra
9. Eye Contact Partners	6–8	Perimeter and Area	Geometry
10. Feedback Check-Ins Figures 3.10 and 3.11	3–5	Fractional Parts	Number and Operations—Fractions
11. Feedback Focused Group Discourse	6–8	Patterns	Operations and Algebraic Thinking
12. Feedback Sandwich Figure 3.12	6–8	Scatterplots	Statistics and Probability

FACT and Figure	Grade-Level Example	Concept(s)	Mathematics Domain
13. Find Someone Who Figure 3.13	6–8	Volume of a Cylinder	Geometry
14. Fingers Under Chin Figure 3.14	K–2	Number Sentences	Algebra
15. Flip the Question Figure 3.15	6–8	Area of a Triangle	Geometry
15. Flip the Question Figure 3.15	3–5	Mean	Statistics and Probability
15. Flip the Question Figure 3.15	3–5	Common Factors	Operations and Algebraic Thinking
15. Flip the Question Figure 3.15	9–12	Quadratic Equations	Algebra
16. Four Corners Jigsaw Figure 3.16	9–12	Proportional Relationships	Functions
17. Gallery Walk	3–5	Two Digit Multiplication	Number and Operations in Base 10
18. Group Frayer Model Figures 3.17, 3.18, and 3.19	6–8	Irrational Numbers	The Number System
19. Group Talk Feedback Figure 3.20	9–12	Sample Size	Statistics and Probability
20. Homework Card Sort Figure 3.21	9–12	Multiplying Polynomials	Algebra

(Continued)

Table 2.1 (Continued)

EACT and Figure	Grade-Level Example	Concept(s)	Mathematics Domain
21. I Think–I Rethink	6–8	Division of Fractions	Number and Operations—Fractions
22. Interactive Whole-Class Card Sorting	K–2	Triangles	Geometry
23. Learning Intentions	K–12	Measurement	Measurement and Data
24. Learning Intentions Reflection Figure 3.22	6–8	Ratio	Ratios and Proportional Relationship
25. Let's Keep Thinking	6–8	Probability	Statistics and Probability
26. Lines of Agreement	6–8	Fractions and Decimals	Number and Operations—Fractions
26. Lines of Agreement	9–12	Quadratic and Exponential	Functions
27. Most and Least Sure About	3–5	Area	Geometry
28. Now Ask Me a Question	6–8	Parallelograms	Geometry
29. Partner Strategy Rounds Figure 3.23	9–12	Order of Operations	Algebra
30. Plus–Delta Figure 3.24	9–12	Pi as a Ratio	Geometry
31. PMI (Plus–Minus–Interesting) Figure 3.25	6–8	Volume and Surface Area	Geometry
32. Questioning Cue Cards Figure 3.26	3–5	Rounding Remainders	Number and Operations in Base 10

FACT and Figure	Grade-Level Example	Concept(s)	Mathematics Domain
33. Ranking Tasks Figure 3.27	9–12	Rate of Change	Algebra
33. Ranking Tasks Figure 3.28	6–8	Numerical Expressions	Number Systems
34. RAQ (Revise, Add, Question) Feedback	9–12	Linear Modeling	Algebra
35. Reflect Aloud Figure 3.29	6–8	Area of a Triangle	Geometry
36. Reflect Then Self-Assess Figure 3.30	3–5	Decimal Addition	Number and Operations in Base 10
37. "Rules That Expire" Probes Figure 3.31	6–8	Operations With Negative Numbers	Number and Operations in Base 10
38. Seeing Structure Figure 3.32	3–5	Distributive Property	Number and Operations in Base 10
38. Seeing Structure Figure 3.33	9–12	Data and Correlation	Statistics and Probability
39. Slide Sort Figures 3.34 and 3.35	9–12	Parallelograms and Proof	Geometry
40. Sort Envelopes Figures 3.36 and 3.37	K–2	Tens	Counting and Cardinality
41. Structures for Taking Action Figure 3.38	3–5	Metric Units	Measurement and Data

(Continued)

Table 2.1 (Continued)

FACT and Figure	Grade-Level Example	Concept(s)	Mathematics Domain
42. Success Indicators	K–2	Partial Sum	Number and Operations in Base 10
42. Success Indicators	3–5	Distributive Property	Number and Operations in Base 10
42. Success Indicators	6–8	Proportions	Ratios and Proportional Relationships
42. Success Indicators	9–12	Rational and Irrational Numbers	Number and Quantity
43. Success Indicator Problem Generating	3–5	Comparing Decimals	Number and Operations—Fractions
44. Take Stock	6–8	Writing Equations	Operations and Algebraic Thinking
45. Talk Moves Figures 3.39 and 3.40	K–2	Solving Subtraction Stories	Operations and Algebraic Thinking
46. Thermometer Feedback	9–12	Probability	Statistics and Probability
47. Traffic Light Sliders Figure 3.41	K–2	Bar Graphs	Measurement and Data
48. VDR (Vote Discuss, Revote) Figure 3.42	6–8	Parallelograms	Geometry
49. What Stuck With You Today?	6–8	Types of Graphs	Measurement and Data
50. X Marks the Spot Figures 3.43 and 3.44	6–8	Ratio	Ratios and Proportional Relationships

Table 2.2   Examples of FACTs Linked to Mathematical Practices

FACT and Figure	1. Make sense of problems and persevere in solving them.	2. Reason abstractly and quantitatively.	3. Construct viable arguments and critique the reasoning of others.	4. Model with mathematics.	5. Use appropriate tools strategically.	6. Attend to precision.	7. Look for and make use of structure.	8. Look for and express regularity in repeated reasoning.
1. Comment Coding	X	X	X	X	X	X	X	X
2. Concept Mix-Up Probes Figure 3.1			X			X	X	
3. Confidence Level Assessment (CLA) Figure 3.2	X	X	X	X	X	X	X	X
4. Conjecture Cards Figures 3.3 and 3.4			X			X		
5. Cover-Up	X	X	X	X	X	X	X	X
6. Enhanced Multiple Choice Figure 3.5		X	X			X		
7. Error Analysis			X	X		X		X
8. Enhanced Sticky Bars Figures 3.6, 3.7, 3.8, and 3.9			X	X				
9. Eye Contact Partners	X	X	X	X	X	X	X	X

(Continued)

Table 2.2 (Continued)

FACT and Figure	1. Make sense of problems and persevere in solving them.	2. Reason abstractly and quantitatively.	3. Construct viable arguments and critique the reasoning of others.	4. Model with mathematics.	5. Use appropriate tools strategically.	6. Attend to precision.	7. Look for and make use of structure.	8. Look for and express regularity in repeated reasoning.
10. Feedback Check-Ins Figures 3.10 and 3.11	X	X	X	X	X	X	X	X
11. Feedback Focused Group Discourse	X	X	X	X	X	X	X	X
12. Feedback Sandwich Figure 3.12	X	X	X	X	X	X	X	X
13. Find Someone Who Figure 3.13	X			X				
14. Fingers Under Chin Figure 3.14	X	X	X	X	X	X	X	X
15. Flip the Question Figure 3.15		X						
16. Four Corners Jigsaw Figure 3.16		X	X			X		

24

Strategy									
17. Gallery Walk	X	X	X	X	X	X	X	X	X
18. Group Frayer Model Figures 3.17, 3.18, and 3.19			X		X	X	X	X	X
19. Group Talk Feedback Figure 3.20	X	X	X	X	X	X	X	X	X
20. Homework Card Sort Figure 3.21	X	X	X	X	X	X	X	X	X
21. I Think–I Rethink	X	X	X	X	X	X	X	X	X
22. Interactive Whole-Class Card Sorting			X		X			X	
23. Learning Intentions	X	X	X	X	X	X	X	X	X
24. Learning Intentions Reflection Figure 3.22	X	X	X	X	X	X	X	X	X
25. Let's Keep Thinking	X	X	X	X	X	X	X	X	X
26. Lines of Agreement					X			X	
27. Most and Least Sure About				X			X	X	X
28. Now Ask Me a Question	X	X	X	X	X	X	X	X	X
29. Partner Strategy Rounds Figure 3.23			X				X	X	X
30. Plus–Delta Figure 3.24	X	X	X	X	X	X	X	X	X

(Continued)

Table 2.2 (Continued)

EACT and Figure	1. Make sense of problems and persevere in solving them.	2. Reason abstractly and quantitatively.	3. Construct viable arguments and critique the reasoning of others.	4. Model with mathematics.	5. Use appropriate tools strategically.	6. Attend to precision.	7. Look for and make use of structure.	8. Look for and express regularity in repeated reasoning.
31. PMI (Plus–Minus–Interesting) Figure 3.25		X	X	X		X		
32. Questioning Cue Cards Figure 3.26	X	X	X	X	X	X	X	X
33. Ranking Tasks Figures 3.27 and 3.28		X						
34. RAQ (Revise, Add, Question) Feedback				X				
35. Reflect Aloud Figure 3.29	X	X	X	X	X	X	X	X
36. Reflect Then Self-Assess Figure 3.30	X							
37. "Rules That Expire" Probes Figure 3.31		X					X	X
38. Seeing Structure Figures 3.32 and 3.33	X							X

#	Technique	1	2	3	4	5	6	7	8
39.	Slide Sort Figures 3.34 and 3.35			X	X	X	X	X	X
40.	Sort Envelopes Figures 3.36 and 3.37	X	X	X	X	X	X	X	X
41.	Structures for Taking Action Figure 3.38	X	X	X	X	X	X	X	X
42.	Success Indicators	X	X	X	X	X	X	X	X
43.	Success Indicator Problem Generating	X	X	X	X	X	X	X	X
44.	Take Stock	X	X	X	X	X	X	X	X
45.	Talk Moves Figures 3.39 and 3.40	X	X	X	X	X	X	X	X
46.	Thermometer Feedback	X							
47.	Traffic Light Sliders Figure 3.41	X							
48.	VDR (Vote, Discuss, Revote) Figure 3.42	X	X	X	X	X	X	X	X
49.	What Stuck With You Today?	X	X	X	X	X	X	X	X
50.	X Marks the Spot Figures 3.43 and 3.44	X	X	X	X	X	X	X	X

Chapter 3

Get the FACTs! Formative Assessment Classroom Techniques

The 50 FACTs selected for this chapter were gathered from a variety of sources. Several of the FACTs included in this chapter were practiced and honed by the authors during their combined 25 years as middle and high school teachers and 35 years supporting the professional learning of mathematics and science teachers. Some FACTs were originally developed and used as professional development strategies for adult learners. Others have been gleaned from the literature on formative assessment. Classroom teachers have also contributed ideas for several of the FACTs in this chapter. Each FACT selected for inclusion in this chapter was reviewed with respect to the following considerations:

1. Does the FACT elicit information or provide evidence about students' understanding of the core ideas, concepts, or practices of mathematics?

2. Does the FACT appeal to students? Would students want to respond to the assessment technique?

3. Can the FACT be used in a variety of classroom configurations, including individual work, small-group discussion, and whole-class discourse?

4. Can the FACT be used flexibly in a range of classroom environments and with a variety of student populations?

5. Does the FACT promote the spirit of inquiry and intellectual curiosity about ideas and processes in mathematics?

6. Is the FACT easy to use? Can it be easily administered and responded to, and is it time efficient? Are the materials readily available? Can that data be quickly collected and analyzed?

7. Does the FACT have reciprocal benefits? Is it as beneficial to students in supporting their learning as it is for teachers in informing instruction and improving teaching practice?

8. Will the FACT make a difference in the classroom learning environment? Will it support a culture of sharing ideas and seeking understanding?

9. Will instruction and opportunities to learn improve or be enhanced when the FACT is used?

10. Does the FACT support achievement of learning standards and key ideas in mathematics? Can the FACT be used to support mathematical practices and processes? Can the FACT be used to support the integration of literacy capacities with mathematics? Can the FACT be used with any state's standards, regardless of whether or not it has adopted the Common Core State Standards?

Now it is time to get the FACTs!

FACT 1

COMMENT CODING

Description

Comment Coding is used to provide feedback to students that will encourage them to improve their work and reconsider or expand on their thinking. In a study described in the book *Assessment for Learning* (Black, Harrison, Lee, Marshall, & Wiliam, 2003), randomly selected students were given a task to complete and then received one of three types of feedback. The first group received tailored, written comments only; the second group received marks only (answers marked right or wrong, often accompanied by a grade); and the third group received both marks and comments. On subsequent tasks in which students could improve their work after the teacher returned it to the students, the students who received comments only performed better than the other two groups. The research indicates that feedback emphasizing only ways to improve versus feedback that passes judgment on students' abilities (marks and grades), even though comments were provided with the marks in the third group, is more effective at encouraging students to consider and use feedback for improvement. Receiving such feedback is an important and necessary part of the learning process. Once students are familiar with this type of feedback, teachers can use *Comment Coding* to expedite the written commenting process when providing comments on work for all students.

How This FACT Promotes Student Learning

Providing feedback to students in a nonjudgmental way rather than marking and grading their work has been shown to improve student learning. When students receive a marked-up or graded paper, even when comments are included, they may feel that they are not "good at math" and fail to use the comments to improve their work. Additionally, students who receive a good grade, but can still improve, will often ignore the comments because they feel their work is "good enough." Providing only the comments they need to improve, without marks and grades, constructively engages students in using feedback to make progress toward meeting a learning goal.

How This FACT Informs Instruction

The primary purpose of this FACT is to provide feedback to students so they can improve their work and revise ways of thinking about mathematical concepts and procedures. If students are beginning to learn concepts and new skills it is not fair, nor is it beneficial to their learning, to pass judgment by giving them a grade on their work when they do not yet have a full grasp of the material. Seeing the difference in learning attitudes and performance when the *Comment Coding* FACT is used helps teachers break the habit of marking up and grading every piece of work, especially during formative stages of teaching and learning. Instead, teachers can focus on using comment codes for feedback, giving students an opportunity to improve their work and revise their thinking while they are still developing a conceptual understanding and before they are ready to be summatively assessed.

Design and Administration

Create a bank of comments for written feedback. As you build a bank of comments, consider creating a poster of codes for common comments and feedback prompts and add new codes as needed. The codes you create can be used by students or by the teacher to save time when making comments on student work. The teacher does not always have to be the source of the comments. Have students work in groups to provide comments on other students' work. The following are some examples of codes that can be used with this FACT:

Unclear Procedure (UP): Not clear what procedure you used.

Insufficient Evidence (IE): Not enough evidence to support your ideas.

Evidence Inappropriate (EI): Evidence is not appropriate for your conjecture.

Met *Success Indicator* (SI1, SI2, SI3): This section provides evidence of meeting one (or two or three) of the indicators for success.

Measurement Error (ME): You have a measurement error here.

Computation Error (CE): You have a computational error here.

Use Word Wall (WW): Incorporate words from our unit word wall.

Incorrect Word (IW): Incorrect use of a mathematics term; can you find a different word to use?

Go Visual (GV): A representation would help support your explanation.

Data Display (DD): The data you included are appropriate, but can you think of a better way to display the data?

Confused Concept (CC): I think you confused this with a different concept.

Missing Principle or Concept (MP or MC): You seem to be missing a mathematics principle (or concept) we discussed in class.

Explain Reasoning (ER): Your reasoning is unclear.

Rethink (R): You might want to rethink whether this makes sense based on what we did in class.

Show Work (SW): Show all the steps to your solution.

Flawed Reasoning (FR): Can you identify the flaw in your reasoning?

Different Approach (DA): Can you find a different way to solve this?

Use a Representation (UR): Think of a representation you can use to explain this.

Relate Method (RM): Explain how your method relates to this problem.

More Precision (MP): Be more precise here.

For example, when constructing a graph from data students collected and using it to explain what the data show, a teacher might use feedback codes such as label axis (LA), needs title (NT), check your scale (CS), check accuracy of points plotted (PP), use a different type of graph (DG), start at zero (SZ), check the data (CD), check how your line or curve is drawn (CL), clarify comparisons (CC), explain trend (ET), check your correlation (CC), and justify your conclusion (JC).

Connection to Mathematics Standards

This FACT can be used to provide students with feedback on their understanding of any mathematical key ideas in the standards. The example shows how this FACT can be used for constructing and analyzing graphs. It can also be used with any of the mathematical practices.

General Implementation Attributes

Ease of Use: Medium   **Time Demand:** High   **Cognitive Demand:** Medium

Modifications

This FACT can be combined with *Two Stars and a Wish* (Keeley & Tobey, 2011) by providing two positive comments and a comment that points out an area of improvement. It can also be linked to *Learning Intentions* (FACT 23) and *Success Indicators* (FACT 42). Consider adding a unit specific anchor chart next to the *Comment Code* poster to track common difficulties specific to the unit content. In addition to the codes you develop, have students come up with codes that can be used for feedback on their work.

Caveats

The comments you provide are useful only if they are substantive enough to provide guidance for students to improve their work or revise their thinking without actually doing the work or thinking for the student. Avoid vague comments such as "Good job here," "You could improve here," "Be careful with your conclusion," "Use a better explanation," "Your thinking is incorrect," and symbols such as smiling ☺ and sad ☺ faces. They do little to provide useful feedback. Additionally, it is not helpful to explicitly point out to a student that they have a misconception and correct it for them. Provide a comment that will instead encourage them to rethink their idea or consider an alternative explanation or solution.

When this FACT is initially used, be aware that students may not like it. They are used to getting back papers that have been marked and graded. Also, be aware that feedback may not be interpreted by the student in the way you intended.

This FACT does not mean that grading/marking should not be used. Once students have had an opportunity to learn, practice, and improve their work and are ready to submit their work for review or judgment (such as a grade), then it's certainly important to document the extent to which they have met the learning target by assigning a summative grade and marking their work.

Use With Other Disciplines

This FACT can also be used in science, social studies, language arts, health, foreign languages, and visual and performing arts. Consider creating a bank of codes used for *Comment Coding* that can be used with each of the disciplines.

My Notes

_____

_____

_____

_____

_____

FACT 2

CONCEPT MIX-UP PROBES

Description

Concept Mix-Up Probes are two-tiered formative assessment probes that elicit students' ideas about frequently confused concepts. These concepts are often confusing because of the similarity in the words or contexts used. Use of this FACT can reveal whether students confuse one concept with another.

How This FACT Promotes Student Learning

Concept Mix-Up Probes provide an opportunity for students to grapple with a concept by considering the words used to describe a concept or the context in which the concept is used. It also helps students recognize the specialized language used in mathematics.

How This FACT Informs Instruction

Concept Mix-Up Probes reveal whether students confuse two or more concepts either because they lack conceptual understanding of one or both concepts or different contexts contribute to misunderstanding. Figure 3.1 is an example of an algebraic *Concept Mix-Up Probe* that reveals how a concept can be confused with other concepts. In this example, students may mix up the concept of an expression with the concept of a unit and/or slope and select D, G, and/or H along with other selections that are true or false about the use of expressions. Information about students' thinking related to the concept is used to inform instructional decisions that address both the precise language used to communicate concepts in mathematics and the conceptual understanding students need to distinguish between different concepts and contexts.

Design and Administration

Select two or more different concepts that use similar words or symbols or in which the words or symbols are used differently within similar contexts. Develop distracters based on common ways students mix up the concepts in mathematics. For example, the first part of a *Concept Mix-Up Probe* can focus on terms such as perimeter and area; average and mean; ratio and rate; variables and other uses of letters in mathematics; number, numeral, and digit; and evaluate, simplify, and solve. The second part of

Figure 3.1 Example of an Algebraic Expressions *Concept Mix-Up Probe*

Is It True?

If $m = 5$, circle all the statements below that are true for the expression $3m$.

 A. $3m = 35$

 B. $3m = 8$

 C. $3m = 3 + 5$

 D. $3m = 3$ meters

 E. $3m = 15$

 F. $3m = 3$ times 5

 G. $3m$ means the slope is $\frac{3}{5}$

 H. $3m = 3$ miles

Explain your reasoning for each circled statement:

Source: Tobey, C. R., & Arline, C. (2009). *Uncovering student thinking in mathematics, grades 6–12: 30 formative assessment probes for the secondary classroom* (p. 180). Thousand Oaks, CA: Corwin. Used with permission.

the probe asks students to explain their reasoning using the words or concepts. This FACT can be used as an elicitation prior to a lesson to gauge the extent to which students know and can use the mathematics terminology, symbols, and concepts they will encounter during instruction.

Connection to Mathematics Standards

This FACT can be used to target concepts, symbols, and vocabulary that make up key ideas in the mathematics standards. The example shows how the FACT is used with algebraic expressions. The mathematical practices of constructing viable arguments and attending to precision are enhanced when students can distinguish between concepts in similar contexts and use mathematics terminology with precision.

General Implementation Attributes

Ease of Use: High   **Time Demand:** Medium   **Cognitive Demand:** Medium

Modifications

Reverse the probe's prompt and answer choices by developing a prompt that provides a description or an example of a concept and have students choose the word or concept that best matches the description or example.

Caveats

This probe is most effective if students have had prior instruction related to the concepts. The second part of this probe is the most important—do not overlook it if students select the correct response. Students can select an answer and still demonstrate a lack of conceptual understanding in their explanation. Be aware that this FACT may be challenging for English language learners (ELLs) because sometimes the words we use in mathematics have a different translation in their language.

Use With Other Disciplines

This FACT can also be used in science, social studies, language arts, health, foreign languages, and visual and performing arts. For instance, in social studies the "L" words of *latitude* and *longitude* are frequently mixed up when students use them to read maps.

My Notes

_____

_____

_____

_____

_____

FACT 3

CONFIDENCE LEVEL ASSESSMENT (CLA)

Description

Confidence Level Assessment (CLA) is used to assess students' level of confidence on a particular task or assessment item. *CLAs* can be used to determine students' readiness to proceed with a task. *CLAs* can also be used to assess students' confidence in their answer choice(s) on formative assessment items such as probes or from question banks. The information can be quickly reviewed by the teacher to inform next steps in supporting students' learning related to completing the task, understanding of mathematical concepts or practices, or readiness for summative assessment.

How This FACT Promotes Student Learning

CLAs provide students with a metacognitive opportunity to self-assess the extent to which they feel confident in completing their task or how confident they are in their answer choices on assessment items. It is important for students to have confidence in their ability to undertake a task, as well as confidence in their answers and ways of thinking. Uncertainty or lack of confidence is a self-assessment feedback signal to the student that he or she may need additional help with completing a task or understanding the content of a lesson.

How This FACT Informs Instruction

CLAs help the teacher identify areas where students feel they can proceed with a task or understand the content that has been taught. High confidence in the ability to complete a task is an indication that the teacher can proceed with the lesson. Low confidence indicates a need to further prepare students for the task at hand. *CLAs* prior to a task can be used to assign small groups so that there is at least one person in a group who is confident in proceeding and can help others.

For example, after teaching the concept of multiplication, the teacher might use *CLAs* to ascertain how confident students are in developing an array model they can use to demonstrate and explain the difference between the factors and the product.

CLAs also indicate the extent to which students believe their answers to a formative assessment probe or set of formative assessment questions are correct. Low confidence levels may signal the need for additional instruction to advance students' learning. Medium and high confidence levels on correct answer choices can be an indication of readiness for summative assessment. High confidence in a wrong answer to a conceptually based question is a signal to the teacher that the student may have a strongly held misconception that cannot merely be corrected but may need to be addressed through instructional strategies that support conceptual change.

Design and Administration

Establish a confidence scale such as 0 to 3: 0—no confidence and/or simply a guess with no understanding; 1—low confidence; 2—medium confidence; 3—high confidence. When using *CLAs* with tasks or activities that are part of the day's lesson, ask students to hold up fingers (closed fist, 1 finger, 2 fingers, 3 fingers) to indicate how confident they are in being able to move into the task or activity. If students are being prepared for a task and activity that will commence the next day, use *CLAs* as an exit slip and have the students describe why they feel confident or unconfident and what they need to proceed with the task. This added writing piece provides additional formative information the teacher can use to prepare students for the lesson.

If *CLAs* are used with formative assessment items, such as probes, banks of assessment items, or benchmarking practice tests, have students indicate next to their answer what their confidence level is in their answer choice(s) using the 0–3 ranking levels or whatever scale you wish to use. Figure 3.2 is an example of a chart that can be posted in the classroom for use with *CLAs*.

Figure 3.2 Confidence Indicator

Confidence Level	Indicator of Confidence
0	I have no confidence. I cannot proceed with the task. I don't know the answer, or I guessed.
1	I am slightly confident. I can proceed with the task but need some help. I could answer the question using some knowledge or skills, but I am not sure it is correct.
2	I am confident. I can proceed with the task on my own. I could answer the question using my knowledge or skills, and I think my answer is probably correct.
3	I am very confident. I can proceed with the task, and I can help others. I could correctly answer the question using my knowledge or skills, and I can easily explain the answer to others.

Connection to Mathematics Standards

This FACT can be used to formatively assess students' confidence in a task or assessment that targets any of the key ideas in mathematics. The example shows how it can be used to show confidence in understanding multiplication. It is particularly helpful in determining how confident students are in connecting a mathematical practice to a key mathematical idea.

General Implementation Attributes

Ease of Use: High   **Time Demand:** Low   **Cognitive Demand:** Medium

Modifications

This FACT can be combined with the *Human Scatterplots* technique when used with formative assessment probes (Keeley & Tobey, 2011). The *y*-axis represents the answer choices, and the *x*-axis represents a continuum of confidence.

Caveats

Even though students may indicate the highest level of confidence in a correct answer choice or in their readiness to proceed with a task, it is still important to check for their understanding before they assist or explain a concept to others.

Use With Other Disciplines

This FACT can also be used with tasks and assessments in science, social studies, language arts, health, foreign languages, and visual and performing arts. For example in foreign languages, students learn the names of foods. They can be given menus in the language they are learning and indicate how confident they are in ordering items from a menu.

My Notes

_____

_____

_____

_____

_____

FACT 4

CONJECTURE CARDS

Description

The *Conjecture Cards* FACT consists of a set of cards, each card containing a different conjecture about a mathematics idea or problem. In mathematics, a conjecture is a mathematical statement, which may appear to be true but has not yet been formally proved. Students evaluate each conjecture and then select the conjectures that are always true and include the evidence they used to prove it. They may also justify why the other conjectures are sometimes true or never true.

How This FACT Promotes Student Learning

The *Conjecture Cards* FACT provides an opportunity for students to evaluate a conjecture by carefully considering the chain of reasoning that proves or disproves a conjecture. *Conjecture Cards* provide an opportunity for students to identify the types of evidence needed to prove or disprove a conjecture. It also encourages productive mathematics talk and the skill of listening carefully to others as they share their ideas.

How This FACT Informs Instruction

As students discuss the conjectures, misconceptions may be identified, and these can be addressed through the design of activities that will surface and confront students with their initial ideas. Additionally, this FACT helps teachers determine whether students can identify appropriate and sufficient evidence to justify whether a conjecture is true and whether they can use norms and conventions to engage in productive math talk.

Design and Administration

Develop a question that can generate a variety of conjectures. Divide the class into small groups according to the number of cards. Figure 3.3 is an example of using *Conjecture Cards* to formatively assess students' understanding of inequalities and the evidence they use to support whether an inequality is always true when $m > 0$ and $n < 0$.

Figure 3.3 *Conjecture Cards* for "Which Inequalities Are Always True?"

If $m > 0$ and $n < 0$, which inequalities are always true?		
$m + n < 0$	$m + n > 0$	$m - n > 0$
$m - n < 0$	$(m)(n) < 0$	$(m)(n) > 0$
$\dfrac{m}{n} > 0$	$\dfrac{m}{n} < 0$	$\dfrac{n}{m} > 0$
$\dfrac{n}{m} < 0$	$(m + n)(m + n) < 0$	$(m + n)(m + n) > 0$

Distribute a set of cards to each group so each student in a group has one card. Students take turns reading the conjecture on their card to their group and describing the evidence that proves or disproves it. After the student with the card shares his or her conjecture and evidence, others in the group can add to the support or rebuttal of the conjecture. The conjecture card is then placed on a conjecture chart under "always true," "sometimes true," or "never true."

During small-group and whole-group discussion, the teacher listens and notes ideas with which students are struggling. The teacher considers learning opportunities that may be needed to confront students with their alternative ideas, working through them by helping the students identify the evidence that supports a conjecture as well as evidence that disproves a conjecture.

Connection to Mathematics Standards

This FACT can be used to formatively assess students' understanding of key ideas in mathematics. Figure 3.3 is an example of using *Conjecture Cards* to formatively assess how students interpret algebraic inequalities. It also provides an opportunity to use the practice of constructing viable arguments and critiquing the reasoning of others as students provide justification to prove or disprove their conjecture. Students also attend to precision when communicating their ideas mathematically.

General Implementation Attributes

Ease of Use: Medium   **Time Demand:** Medium   **Cognitive Demand:** High

Modifications

Justified List or *Sometimes, Always, Never True* probes can be modified to develop *Conjecture Cards* for this strategy (Keeley & Tobey, 2011). For example, the formative assessment probe *Value of the Inequality*, shown in Figure 3.4, was modified to create *Conjecture Cards*.

Caveats

Make sure students are familiar with conjectures and what constitutes evidence before using this FACT.

Use With Other Disciplines

This FACT can also be used in science (as claim cards), social studies, English language arts, and health. For example, in English language arts, students can evaluate a set of statements based on a story or an article they read. They can support or refute the statements by citing evidence from the text.

Figure 3.4	Example of a Formative Assessment Probe Modified for *Conjecture Cards*

Value of the Inequality

If $m > 0$ and $n < 0$, decide if each inequality is *Always True, Sometimes True, Never True,* or *Can't Be Determined* with the given information.

Circle the correct answer.	Justify your choice.
1. $\boldsymbol{m + n < 0}$ a. Always True b. Sometimes True c. Never True d. Can't Be Determined	
2. $\boldsymbol{m - n > 0}$ a. Always True b. Sometimes True c. Never True d. Can't Be Determined	
3. $\boldsymbol{(m)(n) < 0}$ a. Always True b. Sometimes True c. Never True d. Can't Be Determined	
4. $\dfrac{\boldsymbol{m}}{\boldsymbol{n}} > 0$ a. Always True b. Sometimes True c. Never True d. Can't Be Determined	

Source: Tobey, C. R., & Arline, C. (2014a). *Uncovering student thinking about mathematics in the common core, grades 6–8: 25 formative assessment probes* (p. 94). Thousand Oaks, CA: Corwin. Used with permission.

My Notes

_____

_____

_____

_____

_____

FACT 5

COVER-UP

Description

Cover-Up (Creighton, Tobey, Karnowski, & Fagan, 2015) involves a brief whole-class discussion about the *Learning Intention* (see FACT 23) and *Success Indicators* (see FACT 42) in which students first read and then re-create, in their own words, each component. Notably, the *Learning Intention* and *Success Indicators* are read twice: first, by the teacher, to allow the students to hear and read the components of the learning goal, and, second, by the students themselves. The strategy is based on the idea that having students rephrase the *Learning Intention* and *Success Indicators* in their own words will help them better understand what is stated in the learning goal.

How This FACT Promotes Student Learning

By having students rephrase the components of the learning goal in their own words, *Cover-Up* helps ensure that students understand the goal of their learning and the criteria for gauging success. The FACT draws on multiple modes of learning as students read, hear, and talk about the components of the learning goal together.

How This FACT Informs Instruction

Before teachers can find out what students are learning, before teachers can give feedback, and before teachers can engage students as resources for one another and as owners of their own learning, the learning goal(s) must be clear to teachers and to students (Wiliam & Leahy 2015). Too often, teachers post a learning goal, point it out at the beginning of the lesson, but never check to make sure students are clear about what it is they are intended to learn. A teacher can easily get valuable evidence about what students do and do not understand about the components of the goal(s) for learning.

Design and Administration

The teacher posts the *Learning Intention* (also called a learning target or learning goal) and *Success Indicators* for students to see and reads them aloud to the students, once. Students are then asked to reread the *Learning Intention* and *Success Indicators* once to themselves. The teacher then covers up the *Learning Intention* and asks students to talk with a partner about what they are going to learn and how they will know they have learned it.

When students have had a few minutes to talk together, the teachers asks for volunteers to share one part of what they discussed. The goal is to accurately re-create the *Learning Intention* and *Success Indicators* in the students' own words, so the teacher records, for all to see, the various parts of the *Learning Intention* that are mentioned in students' comments. The teacher continues calling on students to add whatever parts they remember and understand about the *Learning Intention* until everything is included or no additional ideas can be added. This provides important information to the teacher about what elements of the *Learning Intention* do and do not make sense to students and what needs further clarification or discussion.

The teacher then uncovers the *Learning Intention* and *Success Indicators* and points out anything that wasn't included in the discussion, offering further clarification—or asking students to clarify—as needed.

The following example is an excerpt from a sixth-grade classroom where *Cover-Up* is a routine FACT used:

Teacher:	"Let's review our learning intention (LI) and success indicators (SI)."
	(Reads LI)
LI:	Equivalent fractions can be made from any given fraction.
	(Reads through SI)
SI1:	I can create an equivalent fraction based on any other fractions.
SI2:	I can use equivalent fractions to find the distance between any two fractions.
SI3:	I can explain how to create an equivalent fraction for any given fraction.
Teacher:	"Read through these again and get ready to say them in your own words. I will be covering up our chart."
Student:	"I want to get them all this time!"
Teacher:	"You have 30 seconds. Turn and discuss with someone else what the LI and SIs are about today."
	(After waiting) "So who can tell me what the learning intention is about?"
Student 1:	"I can find a fraction based on other fractions."
Teacher:	"You are missing an important word."
Student 1:	"Equivalent?"

Teacher: "Correct, we will be finding equivalent fractions."

Student 2: "And something about finding the distance between two fractions."

Teacher: "More, anybody?"

Student 3: "Something like finding equivalent fractions?"

(Teacher uncovers LI and SIs)

Teacher: "What do you notice about the last SI?"

Student 4: "We need to explain."

Teacher: "Yes, why is that different than the others?"

Student 5: "The others are doing the work, and this one is about our thinking about the work."

Connection to Mathematics Standards

This FACT can be used to formatively assess students' understanding of the lesson specific goals for learning that relate to the key mathematical ideas and practices. The example provided shows how this FACT is used to develop clarity around the lesson learning goal for equivalent fractions. It also provides an opportunity to use the mathematics practice of attending to precision when communicating mathematically while students describe the mathematics they will be learning.

General Implementation Attributes

Ease of Use: Medium   **Time Demand:** Low   **Cognitive Demand:** High

Modifications

For students who have difficulty recalling the components of the *Learning Intention* and *Success Indicators*, the teacher may wish to give them an index card or handout with the *Learning Intention* and *Success Indicators* listed on it. Students can hide or view the *Learning Intention* and *Success Indicators* by turning over the index card or handout as needed.

Caveats

Parts of the *Cover-Up* FACT may be difficult for ELL students who lack an understanding of the mathematics terminology.

Use With Other Disciplines

This FACT can also be used in science, social studies, language arts, health, foreign languages, and visual and performing arts whenever learning goals are made explicit to the students.

My Notes

_____

_____

_____

_____

_____

FACT 6

ENHANCED MULTIPLE CHOICE

Description

An *Enhanced Multiple-Choice* question is a type of two-tiered assessment. The first part includes the question and the answer choices (selected response). The second part is a constructed response in which students are asked to provide an explanation or justification for their answer choice.

How This FACT Promotes Student Learning

The *Enhanced Multiple Choice* FACT promotes learning by having students support their answer choice with an explanation or justification. The very act of constructing an explanation or justification requires students to think through their ideas and use the practices of mathematics. Unlike an open-response question that sometimes yields an "I don't know" or blank answer, students have a range of answers to choose from that activate their thinking. This helps them form a scaffold on which to build an explanation or justification, which not only prevents guessing but also provides an opportunity for students to draw on their prior knowledge, think through their ideas, and use mathematical reasoning to support their answer.

How This FACT Informs Instruction

This FACT yields more information about student thinking than a typical multiple-choice or other type of selected response question can provide. By examining the explanation or justification for a student's answer choice, a teacher can better understand what a student knows or does not know related to a learning target. Sometimes students can answer multiple-choice questions correctly but lack conceptual understanding of the mathematics and use flawed reasoning. Other times they may answer a multiple-choice question incorrectly but have partially correct mathematical reasoning. Carefully analyzing the students' explanations or justifications reveals the reasoning behind their answer choice and helps teachers identify the extent to which students understand the concept being assessed or the misconceptions that may hinder their learning. Teachers can then use this information to make instructional decisions that will move students toward the intended learning target.

Design and Administration

Choose a multiple-choice question that requires conceptual understanding, not a regurgitation of facts or vocabulary. A well-designed, conceptual, multiple-choice question uses distracters (incorrect answer choices) based on commonly held students' ideas. Quality multiple-choice questions found in existing assessments or instructional materials can be turned into an *Enhanced Multiple-Choice* question by adding the second part, which asks students to provide an explanation or justification for their answer. Figure 3.5 is an example of a formative assessment probe from the *Uncovering Student Thinking in Mathematics* series that uses the enhanced multiple-choice format (Tobey & Fagan, 2014). See the Appendix for sources of enhanced multiple-choice probes in the *Uncovering Student Thinking in Mathematics* series.

Connection to Mathematics Standards

This FACT can be used to formatively assess students' understanding of any of the key ideas in mathematics. The example shows how it can be

Figure 3.5	*Enhanced Multiple-Choice* Question

Decimal Division Estimates	
<u>Without calculating,</u> use mental math and/or estimation to determine the estimate for each division problem.	
Circle one:	**Explain your choice:**

1.   **5.4 ÷ 0.6**
 	
The quotient is
 	
  a. between 0.5 and 1
 	
  b. between 5 and 10
 	
  c. between 50 and 100	

2.   **19.6 ÷ 0.05**
 	
The quotient is
 	
  a. between 3 and 4
 	
  b. between 30 and 40
 	
  c. between 300 and 400	

Source: Tobey, C., & Fagan, E. (2014). *Uncovering student thinking about mathematics in the Common Core, grades 3–5: 25 formative assessment probes* (p. 91). Thousand Oaks, CA: Corwin. Used with permission.

used to estimate quotients. It can also be used to formatively assess the mathematics practices of reasoning abstractly and quantitatively, constructing viable arguments and attending to precision when communicating mathematically since the second part of an *Enhanced Multiple-Choice* question asks students to explain their thinking.

General Implementation Attributes

Ease of Use: High   **Time Demand:** Medium   **Cognitive Demand:** Medium

Modifications

With some concepts, students can also be asked to draw a picture or diagram to support their explanation. In addition to providing an explanation to support their answer choice, students can also be asked to explain why they did not select the other answer choices.

Caveats

When developing or selecting questions for this FACT, make sure they are conceptual questions that promote thinking, not memorization, rote procedures, and recall of facts or vocabulary. Multiple-choice questions that elicit low-level factual information or concepts where students have no prior knowledge are not useful for this FACT.

Use With Other Disciplines

This FACT can also be used in science, social studies, language arts, health, foreign languages, and visual and performing arts. The *Uncovering Student Ideas in Science* series is an excellent source of *Enhanced Multiple-Choice* questions for science (see the Appendix for more information on this series).

My Notes

_____

_____

_____

_____

_____

FACT 7

ERROR ANALYSIS

Description

Error Analysis (Creighton et al., 2015) is used for gathering evidence of students' thinking in which the teacher presents the class with a fictitious student response to a problem. The teacher tells students that there is an error in the work and asks them to analyze the work to determine where the reasoning or problem solving is flawed. The fictitious response is designed to highlight a common error or student misconception that the teacher wishes to address with his or her students. This FACT can be used to probe the nature of students' thinking about the problem and to surface any similar misconceptions held by the students.

How This FACT Promotes Student Learning

Error Analysis supports a learning environment where it is safe to be wrong and promotes the message that the teacher is interested in uncovering and understanding students' thinking rather than simply judging the accuracy of their answers. *Error Analysis* helps students develop self-regulation skills as they practice analyzing the thinking and reasoning of others. As they gain experience with this kind of analysis, they can begin to apply it to their own thinking and reasoning. The FACT can boost students' confidence in their own reasoning by providing an acknowledgment that some misconceptions are based on thinking that is correct in certain contexts but may have been applied to an incorrect context—and thus gives credit for the validity of the initial thinking.

How This FACT Informs Instruction

When using this FACT, teachers obtain information about the extent to which students may have the same misconception provided in the response from the discussion that ensues, as students share their analysis of the fictitious response. Some students may pose additional questions, others may make assertions that correctly identify what was erroneous, and still others may make assertions that are themselves erroneous. This information is then used by the teacher to address students' errors and misconceptions.

Design and Administration

Prior to using this strategy, the teacher identifies or creates one or two examples of fictitious and erroneous student work. Students first complete the problem on their own to gain familiarity with it. The teacher can choose whether to project the problem for the class or provide it individually on a handout. The teacher then shows the class a fictitious student response and asks students to think about the approach and reasoning shown in the response (and/or talk with a partner or small group about them). The teacher is explicit that the work contains an error.

The class then analyzes the work, looking for the flaws in thinking and discussing their ideas about the response. The goal of the conversation is to help students understand the nature of the errors or misconception and to be aware of it in their own work.

For example, a teacher wishes to find out more about his or her students' understanding of comparison of fractions. The teacher knows that one common misconception is the overgeneralization of the idea that "the smaller the denominator, the larger the fraction." While this is true for unit fractions (i.e., $\frac{1}{3}$ is larger than $\frac{1}{4}$), students can sometimes extend this rule to all fractions, believing that $\frac{2}{5}$ is larger than $\frac{7}{9}$ because fifths are larger than ninths. So the teacher presents a fictitious student response that says,

> "If the denominator is bigger, the pieces are smaller. So the first fraction has bigger pieces. $\frac{2}{5}$ is bigger than $\frac{7}{9}$."

The teacher then says to the class:

"This student is not correct, although some of his or her ideas are correct.

"What parts of the thinking are correct, and which parts are incorrect? Look at the work on your own at first and then discuss your ideas with your group."

Connection to Mathematics Standards

This FACT can be used to formatively assess students' understanding of key ideas in mathematics. The example shows how the FACT is used to assess how students compare fractions. It also provides an opportunity to use the mathematical practices of attending to precision when communicating mathematically and constructing viable arguments and critiquing the reasoning of others. Students use their explanation to engage in argumentation when conflicting conjectures are presented. It also supports the practice of looking for and expressing regularity in repeated reasoning as students analyze generalizations made by others.

General Implementation Attributes

Ease of Use: Medium   **Time Demand:** Medium   **Cognitive Demand:** Medium

Modifications

For early attempts, consider showing and discussing one student's analysis of the work of another student. Once the class feels comfortable discussing errors together, you might ask students to share their own responses for discussion.

Students with organizational difficulties may benefit from a step-by-step organizer to help them go through an analysis process, such as the sample provided below:

Step 1: Solve the problem. (Teacher provides the problem.)

Step 2: Look at this example of student work. In this example, the student has an error in his or her thinking and work. See if you can find the error. (Teacher inserts Student Work Sample With Error.) What is the student's error?

Step 3: Discuss the error you found with your group. Hear the ideas of others in your group and then write an explanation of why the student's thinking or approach does not make sense.

Caveats

Don't use this FACT too early in instruction when students are learning new mathematics concepts and procedures. Make sure students are familiar with and can use the mathematics they are learning before using this FACT.

Use With Other Disciplines

This FACT can also be used in science, social studies, language arts, health, foreign languages, and visual and performing arts. For example, in science teachers can share a graph of data from a lab experiment and have students discuss the errors in the graph.

My Notes

_____

_____

_____

_____

_____

FACT 8

EXTENDED STICKY BARS

Description

Sticky Bars can be described as the low-tech version of personal response systems (clickers). Students are presented with a selected response question. The answer is anonymously recorded on a sticky note and collected. The sticky notes are then arranged on a chart pad, on the wall, or on a class whiteboard as a bar graph, representing the different student responses (Keeley & Tobey, 2011). *Extended Sticky Bars* adds an additional element: Responses are collected and graphed at the beginning, midway, and at the end of a sequence of instruction, thus allowing students and the teacher to track how the class ideas are changing.

How This FACT Promotes Student Learning

Extended Sticky Bars makes students' thinking visible to others in a graphic display that honors anonymity. It visually shows how students' ideas vary and change throughout the sequence of instruction, starting at the beginning, checking in midway, and adding a final check at the end. By seeing the range of responses, students accept that ideas may differ and that learning involves the process of working together over time to move toward a common understanding. Because the answer is not divulged initially, the FACT is a strong motivator and promoter of thinking. It creates a desire to "find out" as students work toward learning what the best answer is and continuously ponder the question. During the final round of *Extended Sticky Bars*, if a few students still choose an incorrect answer, students have an opportunity to use the practice of mathematical argumentation to discuss and justify what the best answer is.

How This FACT Informs Instruction

Extended Sticky Bars is first used as an initial elicitation to visually determine the range of students' ideas before beginning a sequence of instruction. The data help the teacher make initial instructional decisions and provide a sense of where the class is at the start of a learning sequence. Midway into a sequence of instruction, the FACT helps teachers monitor the extent to which students have changed some of their alternative ideas and are moving toward understanding. The results may show that students have achieved understanding and that the teacher can move on to the next learning target, or results may show that additional responsive instruction needs to be provided. A final set of *Extended Sticky Bars* shows where the class is at the end of a sequence of instruction and can be used for a final reflection and *Look Back* (Keeley & Tobey, 2011) on learning and instruction. Overall, the data indicate how and when the class is progressing toward a common mathematical understanding and if additional instruction or other responsive actions need to be taken to move all students toward the key mathematical idea and best mathematics explanation.

Design and Administration

This strategy is combined with selected response questions that are used to develop conceptual understanding over an extended sequence of instruction; it typically involves a minimum of 2 days (beginning, end of day, and next day), several days, or a week or more of instruction. For example, assessment probes from the *Uncovering Student Thinking in Mathematics* are an excellent source of questions for this FACT (see the Appendix for more information on this resource). Three different colored sticky notes are used for *Extended Sticky Bars.* Students are given a color prior to the first lesson (elicitation phase) and asked to record their answer selection on the sticky note. Remind students to record their own answer, regardless of whether they think it might be right or wrong. Keep the sticky notes anonymous. Collect and quickly sort them into like responses (use a student assistant if needed). Create a bar graph by placing each similar response atop the other. Figure 3.6 is an example of a formative assessment probe used with the *Extended Sticky Bars* strategy (Tobey & Arline, 2014b). The teacher chose the last question (3) to use with this FACT.

Figure 3.7 shows what an *Extended Sticky Bar* graph looks like initially, before the start of a lesson where students analyze pairs of linear equations to determine similarities and differences in their solution sets.

After the graph is posted, summarize the data and discuss the results with students. At this point, do not give students the answer to the question but explain that they will revisit the question again after they have more information, using the *Let's Keep Thinking* FACT (FACT 25). It is important to let students "hang out in uncertainty" and continue to ponder the question during the lesson. Leave the graph posted in the classroom where it can stay as the first lesson addressing systems of linear equations is taught.

Midway into the sequence of instruction, or whenever the teacher thinks students' instructional experiences may have led to changing some of their ideas, provide a different colored sticky note and give students the same question again. Collect the sticky notes and place them on the graph next to their initial responses. Figure 3.8 shows the second part of an *Extended Sticky Bar* graph given midway into the sequence of instruction. Have students discuss what the data show, but refrain from giving the answer. If the class is still not all in agreement about the best answer, plan the remaining part of the lesson or the next lesson or lessons to target

Figure 3.6	Example of a Mathematics Probe Used With *Extended Sticky Bars*

Systems of Linear Equations

Look at the sets of systems of linear equations.

Circle the set with a solution that differs from the others.	Justify your choice.
1. a. $y = 3x - 4$ $2y - 6x = -8$ b. $y = \frac{1}{2}x + 3$ $4y - 2x = 10$ c. $y = -2x + 8$ $3y + 6x = 24$	
2. a. $y = 3x - 4$ $2y - 6x = 5$ b. $y = \frac{3}{4}x - 2$ $3y + 4x = 1$ c. $y = -\frac{5}{2}x + 3$ $5y - 2x = 8$	
3. a. $y = 6x - 4$ $y = 4x + 6$ b. $y = \frac{1}{2}x + 3$ $y = \frac{1}{2}x + 4$ c. $y = 2x + 5$ $y = -3x + 1$	

Source: Tobey, C., & Arline, C. (2014b). *Uncovering student thinking about mathematics in the Common Core, high school: 25 formative assessment probes* (p. 78). Thousand Oaks, CA: Corwin. Used with permission.

Figure 3.7   Initial *Extended Sticky Bars* Class Responses

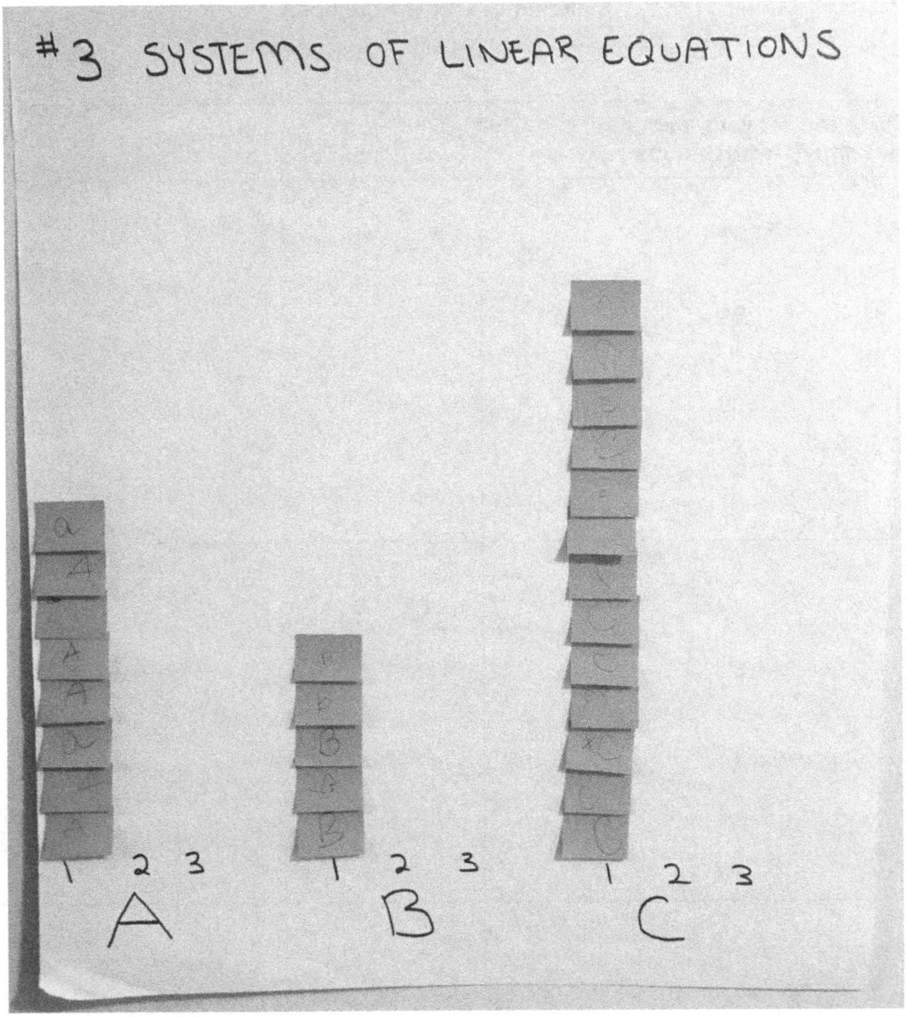

the misunderstandings that remain. You can see in Figure 3.8 that some students are shifting toward the correct answer (B), but most of the class is not there yet.

When you feel confident that students have reached the point where most of the class understands the concept, provide the third sticky note in a new color. Repeat the previous steps. Figure 3.9 shows the third and final round of an *Extended Sticky Bars*. All but six students have moved toward the best answer at this point (B). When there are still a few students who have not moved toward the best answer, engage the class in a

Figure 3.8 *Extended Sticky Bars* Class Responses: Midway Point

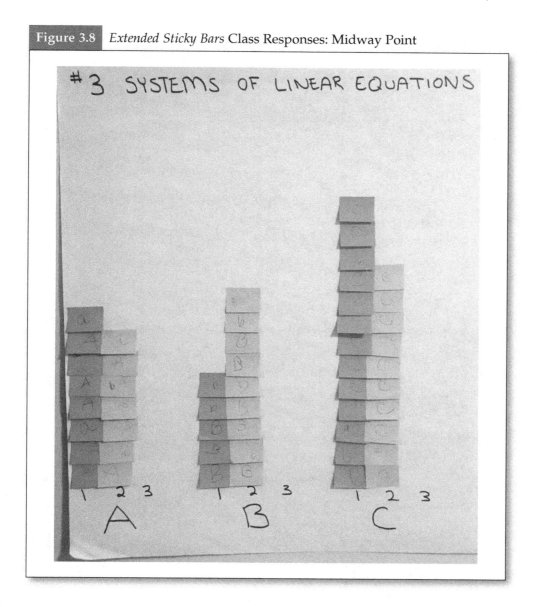

discussion of what the best answer is and why the other answers are not the best answer. For example, students who chose B can present an argument to students who chose A or C about why they think B is the set with a solution that differs from the others. They can explain how B represents parallel lines where A and C represent lines with exactly one solution point. Engaging in evidence-based argumentation to support thinking about the best answer to the question may help these students give up their idea in favor of the evidence-supported explanations provided by their classmates and facilitated by the teacher.

Figure 3.9   *Extended Sticky Bars* Class Responses: End Point

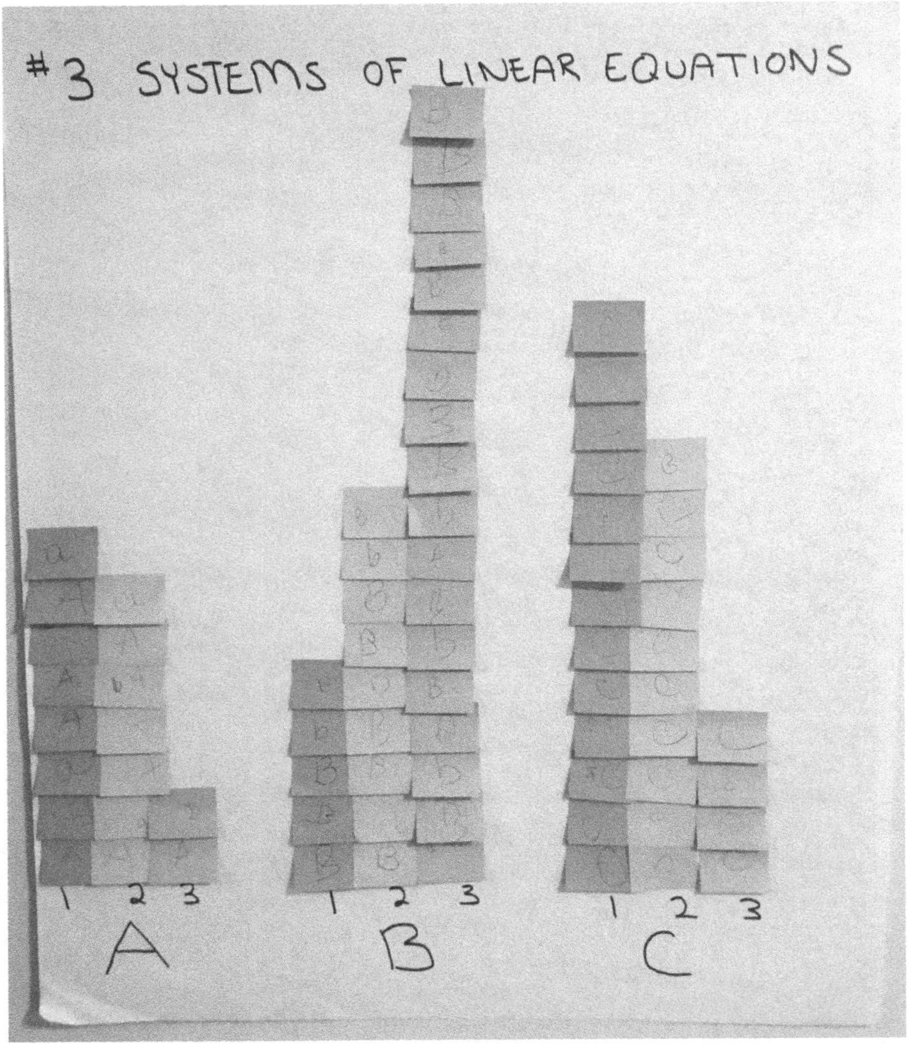

Connection to Mathematics Standards

This FACT can be used to formatively assess students' understanding of any of the key ideas in mathematics and surface common misconceptions or errors related to those key ideas. The example shows how students think about linear equations. It also supports the practice of modeling with mathematics because both students and teachers analyze the graph to determine where the class is in their thinking. When the final answer is presented, students have an opportunity to use the practice of constructing viable arguments and critiquing the reasoning of others as they defend their answer choice and explain why the other answers are not the best choice.

General Implementation Attributes

Ease of Use: High   **Time Demand:** Low
Cognitive Demand: Depends on the question used

Modifications

If you have more than one class, use a different chart for each class. Compare differences or similarities across classes. As a reflection activity, compare the first *Sticky Bars* with the midway and post-instruction bars and ask the class to describe what led them to change their responses. If sticky notes are not available, have students record their response on a slip of paper and create a graph, using a different color and tape for each time the question is posed. Personal response systems (clickers) can also be used if the graph image is captured each time the question is posed, saved, and used to compare to previous results. You can also link this FACT to students' use of data by asking the class to come up with other ways the data can be organized and displayed.

Caveats

Extended Sticky Bars should be used with questions that are followed up with instructional experiences in which students are challenged to change their ideas as they gain additional knowledge and information. DO NOT give the answer to the question after students have provided their response. Let them hang out in uncertainty for a little while so they will discover the answer for themselves during their instructional experiences, even when they are correct initially. To use *Extended Sticky Bars*, choose a question where students' ideas are developed over at least 2 days.

Use With Other Disciplines

This FACT can also be used in science, social studies, language arts, health, foreign language, and performing arts. For example, this FACT can be also used with the science assessment probes in the *Uncovering Student Ideas in Science* series (see the Appendix). An example of how a biology teacher used this FACT with her students can be seen at www.uncovering studentideas.org/resources/tips-and-strategies.

My Notes

FACT 9

EYE CONTACT PARTNERS

Description

Eye Contact Partners is not a FACT per se but a technique used for pairing students for FACTs that involve interaction with a partner. When given the signal by the teacher, a student makes eye contact with another student. Once eyes meet, the match is made and the student moves to work with that partner.

How This FACT Promotes Student Learning

Students need to have opportunities to interact with and learn from other students in paired activities, not just the student they are sitting next to or tend to choose when given a choice option. The process of adjusting and learning to interact with other students is important for both the academic and social growth of students and supports the language literacy capacities of speaking and listening. Unanticipated pairings allow students to hear different ideas and ways of thinking that may be different from or similar to their own.

How This FACT Informs Instruction

This FACT is used by teachers when there is a need to pair students with others with whom they do not ordinarily have the opportunity to interact with in paired work. As students interact in pairs, the teacher circulates and listens to pairs talk, noting the extent to which they understand the targeted concept or practice and how well they communicate their ideas, their interest in the topic, or misconceptions that may need to be addressed through subsequent instructional planning.

Design and Administration

This FACT is not a formative assessment but a novel technique used to group students for an interactive formative assessment task. The following describes how a teacher might explain the use of *Eye Contact Partners* for the first time to a class.

"Now that you have had a chance to think about and write down your own ideas about whether two rectangles with different perimeters can have the same area, I'd like you to share your thinking with a partner. You are going to select a partner using eye contact. It works like this: First, everyone stand up. When I give you the signal, you will look across the room at someone who is not sitting near you, preferably someone you haven't worked with recently. As soon as your eyes meet another student's eyes, go and stand with that person. You can't switch once you make eye contact. Ready, set, look."

The teacher makes sure everyone has a partner and guides unmatched students toward each other. "Now sit with your partner and take turns sharing your thinking about why common-sized pieces are needed. Listen carefully to ideas that are different from your own, and try to come up with an explanation that you both can agree on and share with the class. I will start the timer for 5 minutes and then we will use partner talk to report out to the class. Ready, set, talk." The teacher circulates observing pairs, listening for evidence of understanding or misunderstanding that will inform facilitation of the whole-class discussion and next steps in the lesson.

Connection to Mathematics Standards

This FACT can be used to pair students for discussion related to any of the key ideas of mathematics. The example shows how it was used to group students to share their thinking about perimeter. Depending on the question used, this FACT can be used with any of the mathematical practices. It especially supports the practices of reasoning abstractly and quantitatively, making sense of problems, constructing viable arguments and critiquing the reasoning of others, modeling with mathematics, and attending to precision.

General Implementation Attributes

Ease of Use: High   **Time Demand:** Medium
Cognitive Demand: Depends on the question

Modifications

For younger students, you might use the following techniques to make it easier to find a partner. Have students form a circle and make eye contact with someone across the circle. Once they make eye contact, they stand with their partner outside the circle. The students remaining in the circle can then see who is available. Another method is to divide students into two even lines. You might even predetermine who is in which line to ensure that certain students are not matched. With the two lines facing each other, have students make eye contact with someone across from them and move to the line facing their partner. This FACT can be combined with the *Partner Speaks* FACT (Keeley & Tobey, 2011).

Caveats

For this to be a semi-random pairing, make sure students know that once their eyes lock with another student's, they can't change and look for another partner. Sometimes there will be an odd number of students in the class. To avoid the one, unmatched child feeling left out after even number pairs are formed, pick three names at random for the first threesome, with the understanding that next time other names will be drawn and that they will have an opportunity to do the eye contact exercise.

Use With Other Disciplines

This FACT can also be used in science, social studies, language arts, health, foreign language, and performing arts to pair students for discussion.

My Notes

_____

_____

_____

_____

_____

FACT 10

FEEDBACK CHECK-INS

Description

Feedback Check-Ins are a structured way to check students' understanding to provide feedback and an opportunity for revision. This FACT involves requiring students to check in with the teacher or a peer on one or two key problems within a problem set.

How This FACT Promotes Student Learning

Receiving feedback and being given an opportunity to respond to it is an important and rich activity for the learner. The feedback clarifies the learning goal as well as where the student has met or has not met the goal. If the student has not met the goal fully, the feedback provides guidance on next steps to better meet the goal. By receiving feedback while working on a scaffolded problem set, students are able to consider the feedback and make revisions at key points during practice or application rather than having to revise items at the end of the problem set.

How This FACT Informs Instruction

Teachers who use this strategy support a classroom culture in which receiving and using feedback is considered key to the learning process. By checking in with students on key problems, the teacher has a sense of how the class as a whole is proceeding by looking for patterns across students' responses and can pull together the class for whole-group feedback if needed.

Design and Administration

After determining your *Learning Intention* and *Success Indicators* (FACTs 23 and 42) and selecting a set of scaffolded problems for individual or partner use during the lesson, identify one or two key problems within the problem set that would provide evidence of students' progress toward meeting the learning goal. Let students know which problems are the check-in problems and ask them to create check-in boxes at the top of their page (if using own paper) or next to the problem (if writing on a handout).

When the problem has been completed, the student is responsible for asking for feedback on their work. Figure 3.10 shows that the student has

Figure 3.10   Example 1: Initialed Feedback Box for Selected Problem

3a. $\boxed{CT}$ 5c. $\square$ Sam Smith
                                                     Sect 3.8

1. a. 3 pieces because 12 ÷ 4 = 3

   b. 8 pieces because 24 ÷ 3 = 8

2. Divide because How many ___ is in ___?

3. a. ⊘ = 6

   6 $\frac{1}{3}$ pieces in whole

   1 ÷ $\frac{1}{6}$

Figure 3.11   Example 2: Student Must Check in for Feedback and Revision

4. Partition the number line into twelfths.

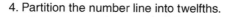

$\frac{1}{2}$ 1

5. What strategies did you use to partition the number lines?

FB $\square$
Check-in $\frac{1}{8}$ is 8 intervals

                  $\frac{1}{6}$ is 6

                  $\frac{1}{4}$ is 4

                  $\frac{1}{12}$ is 12

received feedback on Question 3a. The feedback box is initialed and the student can move on. In Figure 3.11, the feedback box is not initialed, so the student must check in for feedback from the teacher, and then the student must revise and check in again.

Once a student's work has been reviewed and his or her box(es) are initialed, that student can become a reviewer for their peers. In this role, they will gain practice in giving feedback and will initial their peers' boxes.

Connection to Mathematics Standards

This FACT can be used to provide students with feedback on their understanding of any of the key ideas in mathematics, as well as their use of any of the mathematical practices. For example, feedback can be given on students' ability to model with mathematics or their ability to look for and use structure.

General Implementation Attributes

Ease of Use: Medium   **Time Demand:** Medium
Cognitive Demand: Depends on problems given

Modifications

This FACT can be paired with the *Feedback Sandwich* (FACT 12) or *RAQ (Revise, Add, Question) Feedback* (FACT 34).

Caveats

To give effective feedback, students need to understand the components of effective feedback and have multiple opportunities to see the feedback process modeled.

Use With Other Disciplines

This FACT can also be used in science, social studies, language arts, health, foreign languages, and visual and performing arts. For example, in science students can give feedback in solving a sample set of kinematics problems during a force and motion unit.

My Notes

_____

_____

_____

_____

_____

FACT 11

FEEDBACK FOCUSED GROUP DISCOURSE

Description

Feedback Focused Group Discourse (Creighton et al., 2014) is a way for teachers to model how formative feedback is used to move learning forward. In this strategy, teachers revisit the *Success Indicators* after the completion of a task or activity to provide whole-group feedback or feedback on selected student responses.

How This FACT Promotes Student Learning

"It is often helpful to begin any peer-feedback activity with a whole class session" (Wiliam & Leahy, 2015, p. 144). This FACT provides an opportunity to scaffold feedback with a whole-class discussion so that students can be prepared to give similar feedback in peer-to-peer situations. This FACT can be particularly effective in building a shared understanding of the meaning of the *Success Indicators* used to self-monitor students' learning. It helps develop students' ability to use formative feedback to move toward achievement of a learning target.

How This FACT Informs Instruction

By asking students to provide feedback on selected examples, the teacher is able to recognize whether students have a sufficient understanding of the meaning of the success indicator. If they struggle with feedback because they do not fully understand what the *Success Indicator* means, this is an indication to the teacher that clarity is needed. Feedback may also reveal conceptual difficulties indicating to the teacher that students may need additional instruction to complete a task with understanding.

Design and Administration

First, create a feedback poster or anchor chart displayed in a place visible to students with the following sentence prompts:

- You met the success indicator when you did/said _____.
- You didn't meet the success indicator when you did/said _____.
- Here's a hint to help you meet the success indicator: _____.

After students have completed a task, engage them in a feedback conversation using the sentence prompts listed above. The following is an example of what the *Feedback Focused Group Discourse* might sound like as the teacher and students discuss feedback for the success indicator: "I can explain how the way a number pattern grows relates to the way the visual pattern grows.

"I noticed that most of you can explain the way a number pattern grows, but you seem to have difficulty relating it to the visual pattern. Because of this, I want to provide a couple examples of your thinking about the parts of this success indicator before we continue.

"Let's look at this first example (the teacher may name the student or keep it anonymous). Talk to your elbow partner about how this example is meeting part of our success indicator." (The teacher points to the first poster line that reads "You met the success indicator when you said/did _____." The teacher asks for one or two volunteers to share their feedback on how the example meets the success indicator.)

"Now talk with your elbow partner about how this example is not meeting the other part of our success indicator." (The teacher points to the second poster line that reads "You didn't met the success indicator when you said/did _____." The teacher asks for one or two volunteers to share their feedback on how the example did not meet the success indicator.)

"Now talk with your elbow partner about a hint you might give the student so that they can fully meet the success indicator." (The teacher points to the third poster line that reads, "Here's a hint to help you meet the success indicator: _____." The teacher asks for one or two volunteers to share their feedback on how to help the student meet the success indicator.)

The teacher then repeats the process with other samples of student work (if necessary) and ends with having the students review their own work to see how the formative feedback given during the *Feedback Focused Group Discourse* can help them with their own revisions.

Connection to Mathematics Standards

This FACT can be used to provide students with feedback on their understanding of any of the key ideas in mathematics, as well as their use of any of the mathematical practices. For example, feedback can be given on students' ability to model with mathematics or their ability to look for and use structure.

General Implementation Attributes

Ease of Use: Medium   **Time Demand:** Medium
Cognitive Demand: Medium

Modifications

Consider first using a FACT designed to support and build student ability to give and use formative feedback, such as *Peer to Peer Focused Feedback* (Keeley & Tobey, 2011), *Two Stars and a Wish* (Keeley & Tobey, 2011), *Feedback Sandwich* or *RAQ*. Use Think-Pair-Share for the pair talk component of this FACT (Keeley & Tobey, 2011).

Caveats

While observing, monitoring, and supporting students during completion of a task, watch for common issues that arise and choose student work examples to target these issues using formative feedback. If peer feedback is new to students, consider starting with anonymous samples of student work so that students who are emotionally attached to their own work do not view feedback as criticism.

Use With Other Disciplines

This FACT can also be used in science, social studies, language arts, health, foreign languages, and visual and performing arts. For example, in science students may give feedback on the success indicator: "I can develop and use a model to explain the connection between light, reflection, and how we see objects." The feedback may reveal that students can develop the model, but they have difficulty explaining their model.

My Notes

_____

_____

_____

_____

_____

FACT 12

FEEDBACK SANDWICH

Description

To support both peer and self-assessment, the teacher must provide structure and support that enables students to reflect on their own work and that of their peers, allowing them to provide meaningful and constructive feedback (CCSSO, 2008). *Feedback Sandwich* is a technique used to focus peer-to-peer assessment on providing feedback that can be used to move thinking forward. The strategy is designed to help students address for their peers three important questions (Hattie & Timperly, 2007; Sadler, 1989):

What are the mathematics learning goals?

What progress am I making toward the goals?

What do I need to do next to reach the goals?

How This FACT Promotes Student Learning

Receiving feedback and being given an opportunity to respond to it is an essential part of the learning process. The feedback clarifies the learning goal as well as where the student has met or has not met the goal. If the student has not met the goal fully, the feedback provides guidance on next steps to better meet the goal. Research shows that those who provide feedback benefit just as much as those who receive the feedback because the givers of the feedback are forced to internalize *Learning Intentions* and success criteria in the context of someone else's work, which is less emotionally charged than examining one's own work (Wiliam & Thompson, 2006, p. 6).

This FACT avoids the sugar-coated "Bad-News Sandwich" technique in which feedback begins with a positive or supportive statement, followed by a critical statement on how to improve, and then to supposedly make the student feel better about the critical feedback, the feedback ends with a positive comment. There are two dangers to this approach: (1) When certain features of the work are praised, students may overuse those in subsequent work, and (2) by having twice as many positive as negative remarks, it may send a message that the work is acceptable (Wiliam & Leahy, 2015). By ending this FACT with "Next Steps to Consider," it sends a message to the student that he or she should focus on what to do next, not what he or she did in the past.

How This FACT Informs Instruction

Teachers who use this strategy support a classroom culture in which peer and self-assessment are considered key to the learning process. *Feedback Sandwich* provides insight on two levels: (1) the ability of a student to identify attributes related to the criteria for success in others' work and (2) the ability for students to use feedback to make changes to their own work.

Design and Administration

Use with assignments that provide an opportunity for students to demonstrate their conceptual understanding, including solving multistep problems and explaining solution steps, making and justifying conjectures, and providing examples and nonexamples. Make sure to link the feedback to the *Learning Intention* and establish the *Success Indicators* prior to having students complete the task. After the task is completed, pair students to provide each other feedback by having each student complete each part of the *Feedback Sandwich* about the other student's work. Provide time for students to review the peer feedback, discuss the feedback as needed, and then make revisions. A template for this FACT is provided at www.uncoveringstudentideas.org/templates.

Figure 3.12   *Feedback Sandwich* for a Scatterplot

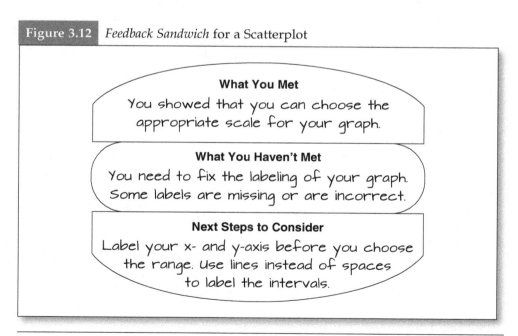

What You Met
You showed that you can choose the appropriate scale for your graph.

What You Haven't Met
You need to fix the labeling of your graph. Some labels are missing or are incorrect.

Next Steps to Consider
Label your x- and y-axis before you choose the range. Use lines instead of spaces to label the intervals.

A copy of this template can be downloaded at www.uncoveringstudentideas.org/templates.

Figure 3.12 shows feedback related to the *Learning Intention*: "How does a scatterplot provide information?" Students created a scatterplot and provided feedback on their graphs for the success indicator: "I can create a scatterplot for a given set of data."

Connection to Mathematics Standards

This FACT can be used to provide students with peer feedback on their understanding of any of the key ideas in mathematics, as well as their use of any of the mathematical practices. For example, feedback can be given on students' ability to decontextualize when solving a problem, or students can be encouraged to use one of the mathematical practices to improve their work.

General Implementation Attributes

Ease of Use: Medium   **Time Demand:** High   **Cognitive Demand:** High

Modifications

This strategy can also be used by the teacher to provide feedback to students or by students to self-assess their own work. For this strategy to be used successfully, teachers must first model the process. Model the process of providing feedback with students by using mock student work or student work from previous years, if available.

After you model the process, use an additional chosen mock or an actual student work example to have students practice providing formative feedback in pairs or individually.

Caveats

This strategy reinforces the notions that the teacher wants students to improve their work and that their improvement is being monitored by the teacher; therefore, time must be provided in class for students to read and react to the peer comments. Whenever possible, provide at least some time in class for students to begin revising their work with clear direction for them to continue on their own. Steer a fine line between prescription and vagueness (Wiliam & Leahy, 2015). If the feedback is too specific, all the student has to do is follow the steps given without having to think. If it is too vague, students aren't sure how to use the feedback. As a general rule, the feedback should always be something students can use to improve their present work as well as use it in future work.

Use With Other Disciplines

This FACT can also be used in science, social studies, language arts, health, foreign languages, and visual and performing arts. For example, in language arts, students can use this FACT to peer assess a students' writing sample.

My Notes

FIND SOMEONE WHO

Description

Adapted from the "getting to know you" strategy, this FACT encourages mathematical discourse. In this strategy, students complete a problem-solving task and then circulate among their peers to find students who used a strategy similar to or different from theirs to solve the problem.

How This FACT Promotes Student Learning

A *Find Someone Who* provides an opportunity for students to examine others' processes and compare them to their own. While examining others' processes, students build on them or add new processes of their own. "Thinking cannot be articulated unless students reflect on the problem and the strategies used to solve it; articulation, in turn, increases reflection, which leads to understanding" (Fennema & Romberg, 1999, p. 188). Often in whole-group sharing situations, not all students have a chance to share, ask questions, and provide feedback due to either time constraints or comfort level. The *Find Someone Who* FACT allows all students to share their own particular strategy and to think about how their strategy is similar to and/or different from other students'.

How This FACT Informs Instruction

Find Someone Who elicits different processes students use to solve a problem. As students are sharing, the teacher can gather information on the range of processes used to determine those to be shared with the whole class. Used prior to instruction, *Find Someone Who* enables the teacher to use the information to plan lessons that move students toward a particular strategy or process. Used during the concept development stage, teachers can use the FACT to gather information to determine students' ability to apply new learning within a problem context.

Design and Administration

Provide students with a *Find Someone Who* handout, such as the one in Figure 3.13, and review the problem to be solved. For example, students might be asked to determine how to make a cylinder from a single sheet of paper that would hold the most popcorn. Would you tape the 8.5-inch ends of the paper together to form the cylinder, or would you tape the 11-inch ends together? Allow students time to individually complete the problem, using the first section to record their processes and solutions. Start by asking the students to find an "eye contact" partner (see FACT 9) by standing up and making eye contact with someone who is not sitting near them (or use other pairing strategies). Ask each pair to choose who will be Partner A and who will be Partner B. Partner A then explains his or her strategy while Partner B asks questions; once that is finished, the roles are reversed. After sharing, the students determine whether they can complete a square (or more than one) on the template. Continue the process with two to three additional partners, adding names to the squares as appropriate. At the end of the *Find Someone Who* process, ask for a few volunteers to share a square on their *Find Someone Who* sheet and explain how their partner used the strategy. A template for this strategy can be found at www .uncoveringstudentideas.org/templates.

Figure 3.13   Example *Find Someone Who* Sheet

My process:	
Find someone who:	
Used a model to solve the problem.	Used the partial products algorithm to solve the problem.
Used the traditional algorithm to solve the problem.	Used estimation prior to solving the problem to check their solution.

A copy of this template can be downloaded at www.uncoveringstudentideas.org/templates.

Connection to Mathematics Standards

This FACT can be used to pair students for discussion related to any of the key ideas in mathematics that involve problem solving. The example shows how it was used in a lesson on estimating the volume of a cylinder. It is especially useful in supporting the practices of making sense of problems and persevering in solving them and modeling with mathematics.

General Implementation Attributes

Ease of Use: Medium   **Time Demand:** High   **Cognitive Demand:** High

Modifications

Students can work in pairs on the problem and form groups of four during the *Find Someone Who* process. The time interval and number of partners can be changed to reflect the complexity of the problem. For less complex problems, a more random approach can be used, with students moving quickly from partner to partner to find strategies that differed from their own in at least one way. You can also use a recording sheet without the boxes labeled about a strategy used. Have students come up with a name or description of the strategy and then explain how their partner used it.

Caveats

This strategy may be difficult for ELLs or students who have a hard time concentrating or hearing. There is a high level of noise in the classroom when many students are talking at the same time. Have them spread out so they may better hear their partners.

Use With Other Disciplines

This FACT can also be used in science, social studies, language arts, health, foreign languages, and visual and performing arts. For example, in science students can find examples of the different ways students solved an engineering problem, reinforcing how a variety of designs are used in engineering to solve problems.

My Notes

_____

_____

_____

_____

_____

FACT 14

FINGERS UNDER CHIN

Description

Fingers Under Chin is a quick, visual anonymous way for teachers to check students' conceptual and procedural understanding. Students face and make eye contact with the teacher while holding zero, one, two, three, four, or five fingers underneath their chin. Fingers represent numbered answer choices, a range of understanding, or other responses determined by the teacher. The teacher can see the individual and class responses, but students cannot since the fingers of their peers seated in front of them are blocked by their bodies. They can't see the fingers behind them without turning around, and unless students have exceptional peripheral vision, they cannot see the fingers of peers seated next to them.

How This FACT Promotes Student Learning

Fingers Under Chin activates thinking and engages all learners in the lesson, since everyone responds. It also provides an anonymous and safe way for students to share their responses, as it is only the teacher facing the class who can see their answer choices. The FACT also creates interest in the range of ideas held by the class, as students wonder how many others chose the same answer they selected as the teacher summarizes the responses for the class.

How This FACT Informs Instruction

Fingers Under Chin helps teachers quickly determine students' answer choices, confidence levels, or other ranges for which the teacher collects class data. The teacher uses the information to inform next steps for the lesson or decide how to group students for further instruction or enrichment.

Design and Administration

Fingers Under Chin can be used in a variety of ways. Fingers can represent answer choices to a probe or other type of assessment question. They can be used for agree/disagree questions (one finger for agree, two fingers for disagree, three fingers for not sure). They can be used to indicate confidence levels (one finger—low; two fingers—medium; three fingers—high). State the question and let students know what responses their fingers will represent. When the teacher gives the signal, all students face the teacher and look directly at the teacher, while holding their fingers under their chin. They must maintain a line of vision with the teacher.

Figure 3.14	Example of an Assessment Probe Used With *Fingers Under Chin* FACT

Equal to 4?

Circle only the math sentences where □ = 4.

a. 2 + 2 = □ – 3   d. □ = 1 + 3

b. 9 – □ = 5   e. 6 + 3 = □ + 5

c. 10 – 6 = □   f. 3 + 1 = □ + 2

Explain your choices:

Source: Tobey, C. R., & Minton, L. (2011). *Uncovering student thinking in mathematics, grades K–5: 25 formative assessment probes for the elementary classroom* (p. 78). Thousand Oaks, CA: Corwin. Used with permission.

This way, they are unable to see their peers' responses. This strategy is used in situations where the teacher needs to quickly collect data from the entire class, but students prefer not to make their responses known to anyone but the teacher. The following is an example of how the formative assessment probe in Figure 3.14 was used with this FACT to elicit students' initial ideas about equality:

"Everyone look straight at me. When I give you the signal, please place your fingers under your chin to indicate your answer choice to the probe. Put a closed fist under your chin if you think none of these are number sentences where the box is 4. Put one finger under your chin if you think one of these is a number sentence where the box is 4. Put two fingers under your chin if you think two of these are number sentences where the box is 4. Put three fingers under your chin if you think three of these are number sentences where the box is 4. Put four fingers under your chin if you think four of these are number sentences where the box is 4. Ready, look at me and hold your fingers under your chin when I give you the signal and keep looking at me until I say fingers down. OK, ready, set, fingers under chin!"

The teacher scans the class for several seconds while students hold their fingers under their chin and maintain looking straight at the teacher. The teacher looks to see how many students chose the best response by holding up four fingers. "OK, I noticed most of you were holding up two or three fingers. Some of you held up a 1 finger and three of you held up four fingers. Well, clearly, we are not all in agreement about how to determine whether 4 makes our sentence true or false. Turn and talk to a partner to share what you think and why, and then as a class, let's come up with a way we can test our answers."

Connection to Mathematics Standards

This FACT can be used to target concepts, vocabulary, or symbols that make up the key ideas in mathematics. It can be used with any of the mathematical practices.

General Implementation Attributes

Ease of Use: High   **Time Demand:** Low
Cognitive Demand: Depends on the question

Modifications

Fingers Under Chin can be replaced with *Response Cards* (Keeley & Tobey, 2011). Use the same technique of eyes on the teacher to maintain anonymity.

Caveats

Make sure students continue looking at the teacher while the teacher scans the class responses. It is important not to break the peer anonymity if the FACT is being used for this purpose. Be aware that this FACT only reveals part of what students are thinking. It reveals the answer choice but does not reveal the reasons for students' thinking. With older students, establish the rule that if they hold up one finger, it is their pointer finger only.

Use With Other Disciplines

This FACT can also be used in science, social studies, language arts, foreign languages, health, and performing arts. For example, in social studies, students can indicate with fingers corresponding to an answer choice which political decision a government should make to address a societal problem. Since this question may surface beliefs some students are uncomfortable in initially sharing with the whole class, the FACT provides anonymity and feedback to the teacher on where students stand with regard to a social issue that will be discussed in subsequent instruction.

My Notes

_____

_____

_____

_____

_____

FACT 15

FLIP THE QUESTION

Description

Flip the Question (Creighton et al., 2014) is a questioning strategy that involves starting with questions of the form "If I give you this information _____, you calculate this result _____" and revising them into questions of the form "If you have this result _____, what information would you have started with?" It can be used both to raise the level of cognitive demand of a mathematics problem and to provide information to a teacher about the extent of a student's understanding.

How This FACT Promotes Student Learning

The *Flip the Question* strategy results in questions that ask students to go beyond just completing a procedure; the revised question often involves analysis as well. Students frequently need to draw on their conceptual understanding of the topic to answer the "flipped" question. Consider the example of finding a set of six numbers with a mean of 8. A student might reason that one possible set of numbers is 8, 8, 8, 8, 8, 8. This student is building on his or her understanding that the mean is a quotient and is drawing on what he or she understands about division. Another student might reason that the sum of 8 and 8 is equivalent to the sum of 9 and 7, so this student might reason that a set of numbers could be 9, 7, 9, 7, 9, 7 and would know the mean is 8 without having to calculate it. Likewise, this student might extend that thinking to reason that 9, 7, 10, 6, 11, 5 has a mean of 8. This student probably understands the mean as a measure of center that "balances" the various values to maintain the same sum of 48 that will be divided by 6 to get a mean of 8.

A flipped question often has more than one correct answer, so flipping a question often requires students to go beyond memorization and solving to comparing, organizing, and/or analyzing. If a student is thinking about questions such as *What is a possible base and height of a triangle with an area of 30 in²?* or *A pair of numbers has common factors of 2 and 4 only. What could the numbers be?* he or she is not solving only one problem; the student is solving many similar problems as he or she tests various possible solutions as well as comparing possible solutions, organizing his or her results and/or analyzing which results are possible and which are not.

How This FACT Informs Instruction

This strategy helps teachers expand their repertoire of questioning strategies for the purpose of finding out what their students know and understand. Because flipped questions often have more than one correct answer, they lead naturally into follow-up questions that provide a much broader picture of what a student knows. For example, a student responds that a possible base and height of a triangle with area 30 in^2 is 6 and 10. The teacher can then follow up with questions like "What is another base and height that also work?" or "Is that the only possible base and height?" or "Is there a largest or smallest number that could be the base or height?" These questions provide the teacher with a much fuller picture of the student's conceptual understanding of the area formula than seeing a student find the area of a triangle with base 3 and height 20.

Design and Administration

The strategy is best suited to questions that are procedural in nature and are of the form "question → resulting correct answer." The revised question embeds the resulting correct answer in the question and asks students to think about what mathematical conditions could have produced that result. Figure 3.15 shows examples of how to ask flipped questions.

Connection to Mathematics Standards

This FACT can be used to formatively assess students' conceptual understanding of key mathematical ideas such as the concepts provided in the examples above. It is especially useful in providing an opportunity for students to use the mathematical process of reasoning abstractly and quantitatively.

General Implementation Attributes

Ease of Use: Medium   **Time Demand:** Medium   **Cognitive Demand:** High

Figure 3.15	Examples of *Flip the Question*
Instead of asking . . .	**. . . the teacher asks . . .**
What is the mean (average) of the numbers 7, 9, 11, 8.5, 7.5, and 5?	What is a set of six numbers whose mean (average) is 8?
What is the area of a triangle with a base of 10 and a height of 6?	What is a possible base and height of a triangle with an area of 30 in^2?
What are the common factors of 32 and 20?	A pair of numbers has common factors of 2 and 4 only. What could the numbers be?
Does the quadratic $y = 2x^2 - 3x + 4$ have a real solution?	What is an example of a quadratic equation that does not have a real solution?

Modifications

Broaden the flipped question to ask about the range of possible solutions. The following is an example.

Original Question	Flipped Question	Broadened Question
What is the area of a triangle with a base of 10 and a height of 6?	*What is a possible base and height of a triangle with an area of 30 in²?*	*How many possible whole-number bases and heights of a triangle with an area of 30 in² can you find?*

Caveats

When thinking about this strategy, be clear what mathematics concepts you want to bring out and what you want students to learn from the problem posed.

Use With Other Disciplines

This FACT can also be used in science. For example, a typical question about density might be, "What is the density of a cube made from unknown material with a mass of 24 grams and a volume of 20 cubic centimeters?" To flip this question ask, "A cube made from unknown material has a density of 1.2 g/cm³. What are a possible mass and volume of the cube?"

My Notes

_____

_____

_____

_____

_____

FACT 16

FOUR CORNERS JIGSAW

Description

Four Corners Jigsaw combines the *Four Corners* FACT (Keeley & Tobey, 2011) with a jigsaw to collaboratively discuss ideas and engage in the practice of mathematical argumentation.

How This FACT Promotes Student Learning

The *Four Corners Jigsaw* provides an opportunity for students to meet with others who have similar ideas to share and discuss their thinking and collaboratively construct a mathematics argument by listening to and evaluating the thinking of others in their group. Students then provide and use feedback to strengthen their groups' argument before presenting their argument in jigsaw groups. The FACT provides an opportunity for students to get feedback from peers on the appropriateness and sufficiency of evidence needed to support their group's argument. When students present their arguments in jigsaw groups, the FACT supports listening skills and norms necessary for productively engaging in argumentation. Furthermore, it provides an opportunity to consider and evaluate the arguments of others, as alternative ideas are presented, which may result in students restructuring their ideas and ways of thinking.

How This FACT Informs Instruction

This FACT provides teachers with an opportunity to identify and examine the different ideas held by the class, first by observing who is standing in which corner. By circulating among the corners while students are sharing their thinking and constructing an argument their group will use to defend their ideas, the teacher gains insight into students' initial ideas and ways of reasoning. As students move into jigsaw groups and present their arguments to students from the other groups, the teacher listens for evidence of changes in these initial ideas and ways of reasoning, as well as the extent to which students use productive mathematics talk and follow established norms for engaging in discussion and argumentation. The evidence gathered by the teacher is used to inform subsequent instruction as well as to provide students with feedback on the quality and strength of their arguments and their ability to engage in mathematical discourse.

Design and Administration

Provide students with a formative assessment probe that elicits three or more ideas, such as the one in Figure 3.16 (Tobey & Arline, 2014a). Or provide a set of statements about a concept in which one statement is mathematically correct and the others are based on commonly held ideas. For example, statements for a *Four Corners Jigsaw* on graphic representations of proportional relationships could be (1) must go through origin and have a constant rate of change that is positive, (2) must go through origin and have a constant rate of change that is positive or negative, (3) must go through the *y*-axis at a positive intercept and have a constant rate of change that is positive, or (4) can go through the *y*-axis at a positive or negative intercept but must have a constant rate of change that is positive or negative.

Begin this FACT by having students individually select the best answer in response to an assessment probe or a statement that is most true about a topic. Have students do a quick write to organize and explain their thinking. After students finish writing, point out the corners or areas of the room that correspond to each of the assessment probe answer choices or the statements (answer choices or statements can be posted at each of the corners). Students move to the corner or area of the room that corresponds with their thinking. They then meet with other students who chose the same answer or statement, to discuss their ideas, clarify their thinking, and collaboratively construct an argument to convince others of the validity of their idea. (*Note:* If corner groups are large, students can split into two or three smaller groups at their corner.)

After all the corner groups finish constructing the argument they will use to present and defend their thinking, students move into the jigsaw

---

Figure 3.16   Example of an Assessment Probe Used With *Four Corners Jigsaw*

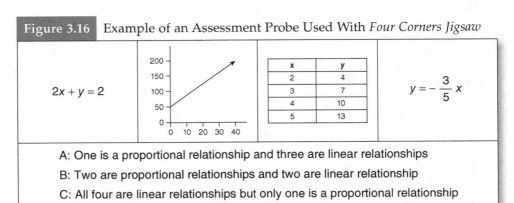

A: One is a proportional relationship and three are linear relationships

B: Two are proportional relationships and two are linear relationship

C: All four are linear relationships but only one is a proportional relationship

D: All four are proportional relationships and linear relationships

---

Source: Adapted from Tobey, C. R., & Arline, C. (2014a). *Uncovering student thinking about mathematics in the Common Core, grades 6–8: 25 formative assessment probes* (p. 114). Thousand Oaks, CA: Corwin.

phase by reforming small groups designated by the teacher, made up of students from each of the different corners or areas of the room. Students in the jigsaw group, each one representing a different idea, share the argument their group constructed. As students listen to the arguments of others, evaluate the strength of each argument, and question and provide feedback to each other, they decide on the "best argument" to share during a whole-class discussion.

Throughout the four corners discussion and presentation of arguments in the jigsaw, the teacher circulates, listening for evidence of mathematical understanding, ability to construct and present an oral argument, how well students use *Talk Moves* and follow preestablished norms for mathematical discourse. During the whole-class discussion of the best argument, the teacher orchestrates feedback to solidify conceptual understanding, or if there are still discrepancies among groups, the teacher plans subsequent instruction that will move students toward the best answer choice or statement and improve their ability to engage in productive mathematics talk.

Connection to Mathematics Standards

This FACT can be used to formatively assess students' conceptual understanding of key ideas in mathematics. It also provides an opportunity to use the mathematics practices of attending to precision when communicating mathematically, constructing viable arguments, and critiquing the reasoning of others, and reasoning abstractly and quantitatively.

General Implementation Attributes

Ease of Use: Medium   **Time Demand:** High   **Cognitive Demand:** High

Modifications

This FACT is not limited to four corners of a room. It can be used with formative assessment probes or statements that include three choices or even more than four choices. Designate areas of the room that correspond to the number of choices. ELLs can be paired with another student from their corner group during the jigsaw to support their oral argument.

Caveats

It is important to establish accepted norms for productive mathematics discussions and arguments prior to using this FACT. See the Math Talk section in the Appendix for resources that support the development of discussion norms.

Use With Other Disciplines

This FACT can also be used in science, social studies, language arts, health, foreign languages, and visual and performing arts. For example, to integrate social studies and writing, a teacher might assign readings from primary or secondary historical texts for students to analyze and interpret. Groups with similar interpretations meet, discuss their interpretation, and collaboratively write an evidence-based argument to defend their interpretation. They then share their arguments in jigsaw groups.

My Notes

_____

_____

_____

_____

_____

FACT 17

GALLERY WALK

Description

Gallery Walk provides a visual way for students to display and communicate their work as well as to receive and provide feedback. Students learn about others' models, investigations, ideas, solutions, or other visual representations of their work and thinking as they walk around and examine the artifacts in the "gallery." As students examine each other's work, they also have an opportunity to provide feedback.

How This FACT Promotes Student Learning

Gallery Walk promotes learning in several ways: (1) Students must think about how to communicate their mathematics work visually, so someone else can look at and understand what is being communicated if the student is not present to explain it; (2) as students examine each other's displayed work in the gallery, they think about their own concepts, ideas, and solutions that are visually displayed and how they compare with others' work; (3) students consider the extent to which the *Success Indicators* for the task have been met and provide feedback to their peers on the quality of their work; (4) students use the feedback provided by their peers to consider how to improve their work; and (5) student thinking is further encouraged when students answer questions posed by their peers during the *Gallery Walk*.

How This FACT Informs Instruction

The *Gallery Walk* provides a visual record of students' mathematical thinking, solution processes, or discussion related to a learning target. Displaying the work allows the teachers to see how different students or groups of students visually communicate their work. As the teacher walks around with the students, the teacher notes areas of difficulty or misunderstanding that may need to be addressed individually or with the whole class, as well as examples of students' work that should be shared with the class. Examining the feedback students leave for one another provides an indication of how well they understand the learning target, their depth of knowledge related to the task, and how well they are able to provide useful feedback to each other.

Design and Administration

Gallery Walks are used when students "go visual" to share and communicate their mathematics work. Assign a task that can be communicated through a visual display. For example, a task may involve displaying and summarizing data from a mathematical investigation; using a diagram to explain a mathematical process; showing a labeled sketch to describe how a mathematical model connects to a context for an problem; sharing a claim, evidence, and reasoning in support of a question; using a graphic organizer to represent one's thinking; or graphing data and analyzing the graph. After students complete their task in small groups, they are given "MTV (making thinking visible) Time" to create a poster or other visual display to communicate their work. When groups are finished, the work is posted on the wall throughout the classroom. Students move from poster to poster with their group, discussing their peers' work (including how it is similar or different from their own group's work) and providing feedback as they examine each poster. Feedback can be recorded on a feedback form and shared during a class discussion or recorded on sticky notes, which are then posted on the visual display.

After the *Gallery Walk*, groups use the feedback generated to discuss what they could do to improve their work (and time should be provided for them to do so). The teacher can also provide a summary for the class of what was similar to or different about each of the displays and facilitate a class discussion to decide on the best way to visually communicate the results of the task. The following is an example of a fourth-grade *Gallery Walk*.

"Now that you have had an opportunity to try different methods of multiplying two digit numbers, you will make a poster to show others two different ways to multiply 23 × 42. Be sure each of methods shows a different way to multiply the numbers. Use arrows and words to show and describe how the methods are related. One person can do the writing, but everyone has to contribute their ideas and agree. I will set the timer for 15 minutes. Make sure someone in your group is watching the time." Six groups of three students each work on their posters.

"OK, now that all groups are finished, come up and get some tape to hang your posters on the wall. Spread them out around the room and stand by your poster after you hang it on the wall." The teacher moves from group to group, distributing a set of sticky notes to each group.

"When I make this sound (teacher claps hands twice), you will move with your group to the poster that is on your right." The teacher points out how to move clockwise. "Each group will visit three different posters— only one group at a time per poster. In your group, you will look carefully at another group's poster and talk about their work. Is it similar to or different from yours? Do you have suggestions for things they might think about or ways to improve their poster? Do you have questions for them? Discuss the feedback or the questions you have about the poster for the group. Designate one person in your group to be the scribe and record your group's comments on a sticky note. Remember how we talked about good feedback and clarifying questions? When your group is done recording on the sticky note, your scribe will sign it with everyone's names and stick it on the poster. You will have 5 minutes for each round. Ready, set, go!" The teacher repeats with the second and third round, each time the group switches to a new scribe when they get to a new poster. On the second and third poster, the teacher also reminds them to look at the comments left by the previous group.

Students finish visiting three different posters and providing feedback.

"OK, now return to your group's poster and read and discuss the sticky note comments and questions left on your poster with your group." Teacher then engages the whole class in a discussion of the comments and questions, sharing the range of comments, questions, and ideas generated by the class. Without going through each poster, pose questions such as "Was there a particular poster that you thought did a great job of representing the group's thinking? Which posters raised questions in your group? Were there any posters that were similar to yours or raised disagreements in your group about what was communicated on the poster?" Have groups take their poster down and, with a different color, make any changes to their work based on the feedback left by their peers. Have them respond to any questions on the back of the sticky note. The teacher can then collect the revised posters, with the sticky notes, for further formative examination to inform next steps in addressing the disciplinary content learning goal, ways to effectively communicate visually, and what constitutes helpful feedback.

Connection to Mathematics Standards

This FACT can be used to provide students with feedback on their understanding of key ideas in mathematics as well as their use of any of the mathematical practices. It especially supports the practice of developing and using a model, because students use a variety of representations to explain their thinking, and attending to precision as students communicate their mathematical ideas so that others can understand what they are thinking. The feedback element of this FACT also supports the practice of critiquing the reasoning of others.

General Implementation Attributes

Ease of Use: Medium   **Time Demand:** High   **Cognitive Demand:** Medium

Modifications

If sufficient time is available, have students visit all the posters. Students can also give a brief presentation to the class, addressing the sticky notes left on their poster. A docent from each group can be assigned to stay with each poster to answer questions from groups.

Caveats

It is important that students know how to provide useful and respectful feedback prior to using this strategy.

Use With Other Disciplines

This FACT can also be used in science, social studies, language arts, health, foreign languages, and visual and performing arts. For example, students can visually communicate ways to use a particular technique in art. Students provide feedback on how well the technique is communicated or feedback on the technique itself.

My Notes

_____

_____

_____

_____

_____

FACT 18

GROUP FRAYER MODEL

Description

The *Group Frayer Model* is a variation of the standard *Frayer Model*, first developed by Dorothy Frayer and her colleagues (1969) at the University of Wisconsin. The *Group Frayer Model* uses a template similar to the standard *Frayer Model*, graphically organizing prior knowledge about a concept or mathematics terminology into four categories: an operational definition, characteristics, examples, and nonexamples (Keeley & Tobey, 2011). The difference between the standard use of the *Frayer Model* and the *Group Frayer Model* is that students work together in small groups to create their *Frayer Model* and that group results are posted on a classroom chart and revisited as group members' thinking changes.

How This FACT Promotes Student Learning

The *Group Frayer Model* is used to elicit students' prior knowledge and provide an organized structure for them to discuss their ideas with peers in small groups. It provides students with an opportunity to initially think about a concept or mathematics vocabulary prior to developing a formal understanding of the concept or terminology, recognize and consider the range of ideas other groups have about the concept or terminology, and revisit their initial ideas after formal instruction to revise or refine their thinking. The *Group Frayer Model* also provides a conceptual bridge between students' operational definition of concepts or words they encounter in mathematics and the mathematical definition.

How This FACT Informs Instruction

Frayer Models have typically been used in a content literacy context for vocabulary development. For mathematics formative assessment purposes they can be used to elicit students' understanding before and/or after teaching a concept so teachers can design responsive instruction that takes into account the ideas students bring to or develop during their learning about a concept or a term used in mathematics. The *Group Frayer Model* helps teachers determine which groups or students may need to be monitored more closely throughout the teaching and learning process as the concept is developed or the terminology is used. The *Group Frayer Model* serves as a record of the initial thinking of the class and is used to design targeted instruction. It is revisited throughout the instructional sequence to help students rethink, refine, and solidify their ideas.

Design and Administration

First, prepare a Frayer Model Chart. Use the *Frayer Model* template, such as the one in Figure 3.17, and keep the chart visible throughout the sequence of instruction (a downloadable copy of this template is available at www.uncoveringstudentideas.org/templates). Write the concept or mathematics term in the center bubble of the graphic organizer. Obtain sticky notes in four different colors. Place one color of each sticky note in each of the boxes of the Frayer chart.

Form student groups of three to four students. Provide each group with a set of sticky notes in four different colors (or squares of numbered plain sticky notes or squares of paper that can be taped to the chart). Show the chart to the students, pointing out the targeted concept or word and explaining what each of the boxes represents. For example, you might

Figure 3.17   Frayer Model Template

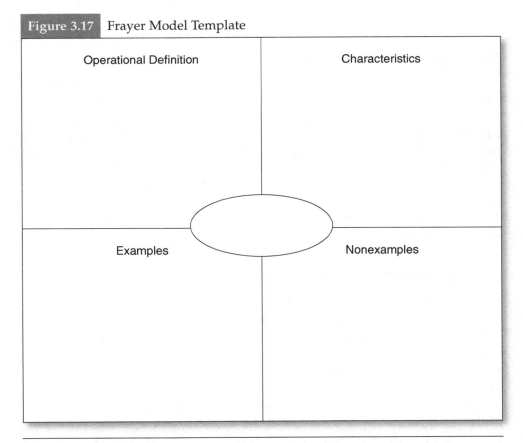

Source: Adapted from Frayer, D. A., Frederick, W. C., & Klausmeier, H. G. (1969). *A schema for testing the level of concept mastery* (Technical Report No. 16). Madison: University of Wisconsin.

A copy of this template can be downloaded at www.uncoveringstudentideas.org/templates.

have to explain the difference between an operational definition (the informal or working definition students use for the meaning of a word or concept) and a formal definition (the mathematics definition of a word or concept). Point out the color of the sticky note or numbered paper square that goes with each box. For example, students write the characteristics on the pink sticky notes or list their examples on the 3 paper square. See Figure 3.18 to see what the posted *Group Frayer Model* chart looks like for the concept of an irrational number before the groups add their colored sticky notes or numbered paper squares to the chart.

Give students 10 to 15 minutes to discuss their ideas for each of the four boxes, related to the concept or word in the middle, and place their agreed on ideas for each box on the corresponding colored sticky note or

Figure 3.18   Group Frayer Model Set Up

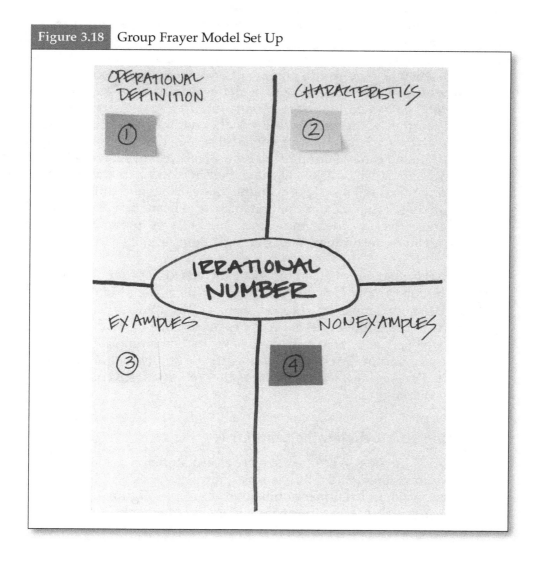

numbered paper square. Each group places its sticky notes or paper squares in the corresponding category, with the members' names or initials on the bottom or back of the sticky note or paper square. For example, a class of seventh-grade students is divided into five groups of four students each. Using the rational and irrational number justified list assessment probe shown in Figure 3.19, students cut out and sort the cards into two categories: rational or irrational numbers (Tobey & Arline, 2014a). After they finish sorting their cards and discussing the difference between rational and irrational numbers, they fill out their sticky notes according to the corresponding color with examples of irrational numbers, nonexamples of irrational numbers (rational numbers), their operational definition of an irrational number, and the characteristics of an irrational number that distinguishes it from a rational number. They then attach their sticky notes to the chart according to the color for each designated box.

When the groups complete the chart, the teacher can get a quick sense of the class and their conceptual understanding. Using the irrational number example, the teacher examines what students think an irrational number is and whether they can distinguish between rational numbers and irrational numbers. Do they recognize characteristics such as irrational numbers can't be turned into fractions and are nonrepeating and nonterminating? Do they understand the ratio of a rational and an irrational number is always irrational? The similarities and differences in group members' thinking can be summarized by the teacher and shared with the class, or each group can be asked to share their thinking with the class as a whole, and the class can be asked to identify similarities and differences in groups' thinking. Using the information, the teacher can then plan instruction that targets the class ideas and monitor for changes in thinking as students engage in opportunities to learn more about rational and irrational numbers.

The chart is then revisited as students gain new knowledge. The operational definition is now changed to a mathematical definition based on how the class now defines an irrational number. Groups are then given an opportunity to revise their original sticky notes or paper squares, showing the difference between their prior and new understanding. The teacher guides a discussion of the changes, culminating in filling out all four sections on the Frayer chart, with final ideas that reflect a class consensus of mathematical thinking.

Connection to Mathematics Standards

This FACT can be used to formatively assess students' understanding of key ideas in mathematics. The example shows how this FACT was used for the concept of an irrational number. For example, Figure 3.19 is used with a *Group Frayer Model* to formatively assess whether students know

Figure 3.19 *Number Card Sort*: Example Formative Assessment Probe Used With *Group Frayer Model*

Rational	Irrational
a. $\sqrt{2}$	b. $\sqrt{25}$
c. $\dfrac{1}{3}$	d. Π
e. $\dfrac{5}{0}$	f. $\sqrt{3} \cdot \sqrt{3}$
g. $\sqrt{2} \cdot \sqrt{5}$	h. $\dfrac{10}{9}$

i. $\sqrt{-9}$	j. $\dfrac{22}{7}$
k. $\dfrac{5.3}{7.2}$	l. $\left(\sqrt{3}\right)\left(-\sqrt{3}\right)$
m. $\dfrac{0}{4}$	n. $0.8\overline{3}$
o. $\dfrac{\sqrt{5}}{\sqrt{3}}$	p. $\dfrac{-8}{\sqrt{7}}$

Source: Tobey, C. R., & Arline, C. (2014a). *Uncovering student thinking about mathematics in the Common Core, grades 6–8: 25 formative assessment probes* (p. 55). Thousand Oaks, CA: Corwin. Used with permission.

that there are numbers that are not rational called irrational numbers. It also provides an opportunity to use the mathematics practices of attending to precision when communicating mathematically, constructing viable arguments and critiquing the reasoning of others as students argue over examples and nonexamples.

General Implementation Attributes

Ease of Use: Medium   **Time Demand:** Medium
Cognitive Demand: Medium

Modifications

This strategy can be used with any of the *Justified List* or *Example-Nonexample* probes or *Card Sorts* (Keeley & Tobey, 2011) or the *Slide Sort* strategy (FACT 39). Students select their examples and nonexamples from the list on the probe or examples on the cards. Depending on the concept or mathematical term selected, you may need to change "Characteristics" to "Features," "Attributes," or "Description" of the concept or word or replace it with "Drawing" or "Symbol" for concepts that can be visually represented. When using justified list or example/nonexample probes with this FACT, invite students to add their own examples and nonexamples in addition to the ones that are on the probe.

Caveats

Make sure students start with an operational definition prior to instruction and end with a mathematical definition when they revisit the *Group Frayer Model* after instruction that clarifies concepts and terminology.

Use With Other Disciplines

This FACT can also be used in science, social studies, language arts, health, foreign languages, and visual and performing arts. For example, this FACT can be used in social studies to explore the concept of a democracy. Students give their operational definition of a democracy, list characteristics of a democracy, and then give examples and nonexamples of countries that have a democracy as their form of government. A list of the countries with and without democracies can be given to students for the examples and nonexamples.

My Notes

_____

_____

_____

_____

_____

FACT 19

GROUP TALK FEEDBACK

Description

Group Talk Feedback is used when students work in small groups to complete an activity or task that involves mathematics discussions. A quick survey instrument provides feedback to the teacher on how well groups functioned and identifies students who may need individual feedback on how they interact with their peers during discussions.

How This FACT Promotes Student Learning

Interacting in small groups is important for achieving learning goals in mathematics. Students learn through the social construction of knowledge. Mathematics talk also supports language development, particularly academic language. *Group Talk Feedback* provides an opportunity for students to reflect on their role as a member of the group and how well the group talk met their learning needs.

How This FACT Informs Instruction

This FACT provides an opportunity for teachers to gather feedback on the effectiveness of a task that involves small-group discussions. It provides an opportunity to collect feedback on how students perceive the effectiveness of group interaction, identify discussion norms that may need to be reinforced, and identify individual students who may need to be grouped in ways that will foster their success during discussions.

Design and Administration

Design a quick survey that students can complete at the end of a group task involving discussion. For example, after observing how multiple trials impacts experimental probability, students are asked to formulate a conjecture. Students in the group have different ideas about how the trial size impacts the experimental probability. One strongly claims that there isn't a pattern because you never know what will happen. Two students agree that the probability seems to be "becoming more stable." A fourth student doesn't contribute to the discussion at all.

Depending on how you will use the data, the survey can be given anonymously or students can record their names. Use the survey to determine class engagement in the discussion, clarity of the discussion topic, contributions, and group process. Use the results to refine the task, modify groups for the next group talk, or give feedback to the class that will improve their small-group discussions both intellectually and socially. Figure 3.20 is an example of a *Group Talk Feedback* form, adapted from the work of Elizabeth Cohen (1994). A downloadable copy of this form is available at www.uncoveringstudentideas.org/templates.

Connection to Mathematics Standards

This FACT can be used to evaluate the effectiveness of group talk in which students discuss mathematical key ideas and use mathematical practices, especially when constructing viable arguments and critiquing the reasoning of others. For students to successfully engage in the mathematical practices in a group situation, they must feel like they can be active, participating members of the group and know that all students are accountable for each other's learning during talk and argument.

General Implementation Attributes

Ease of Use: Medium   **Time Demand:** Medium   **Cognitive Demand:** Low

Modifications

Consider having students codevelop the questionnaire to evaluate group discussions. This can be combined with the setting of norms for productive, accountable talk.

Caveats

For group talk to advance and support learning, students must be clear about the mathematics task, have opportunities to participate, support the participation of others, and feel comfortable being part of the group. Make sure students understand the questions before administering the survey. Honor confidentiality.

Use With Other Disciplines

This FACT can also be used in science, social studies, language arts, health, foreign language, and performing arts. For example, in science students often form small groups to engage in scientific arguments to discuss and defend their ideas. This FACT can be used to evaluate the success of these small-group discussions.

Figure 3.20   Sample *Group Talk Feedback* Evaluation

Group Talk Feedback

Please answer each question honestly. There are no right answers. I want to know what you think so I can improve the next activity.

PART A

1. How interesting was your group's discussion?

_____ Very interesting _____ Fairly interesting _____ Somewhat interesting _____ Not at all interesting

2. How well did you understand what your group was supposed to do?

_____ I knew what to do _____ At first I wasn't sure, but then I understood _____ It was never clear to me

3. How easy was it for you to discuss the topic?

_____ Very easy _____ Fairly easy _____ Somewhat easy _____ Fairly difficult _____ Very difficult

4. About how many times did you have a chance to talk in your group?

_____ 8 or more times _____ 5–7 times _____ 3–4 times _____ 1–2 times _____ None

5. If you talked less than you wanted to, what were the reasons (check off all that apply)?

_____ I talked as much as I wanted to.   _____ I felt afraid to share my ideas.
_____ Somebody interrupted me.   _____ Somebody kept cutting me off.
_____ Nobody paid attention to what I said. _____ I wasn't interested in the topic.
_____ I didn't know enough about the topic. _____ I didn't understand what others were saying.

Share any other reasons here: _____

6. How well did you get along with your group?

_____ Very well _____ Fairly well _____ Somewhat well _____ Not at all

7. How many students listened to each other's ideas?

_____ All of them _____ Most of them _____ Only a few of them _____ None of them

PART B

8. Who did the most talking in your group today?

9. Who did the least talking in your group today?

10. Who had the best idea in your group today?

11. What was your best contribution to the group?

12. Who did the most to encourage and support group discussion today?

13. Would you like to work in this same group again? _____ Explain:

14. What could be done to improve the quality of discussion in your group?

Source: Keeley, P. (2015). *Science formative assessment, volume 2: 50 more practical strategies linking assessment, instruction, and learning* (p. 125). Thousand Oaks, CA: Corwin. Used with permission.

A copy of this template can be downloaded at www.uncoveringstudentideas.org/templates.

My Notes

_____

_____

_____

_____

_____

FACT 20

HOMEWORK CARD SORT

Description

Homework Card Sort uses the *Card Sort* strategy (Keeley & Tobey, 2011) to surface students' understanding of concepts encountered in a homework assignment that involves reading informational text, solving problems, or a mathematics video. Students are given cards with statements or pictures on them that reflect the content in the homework assignment. They sort the cards into different groups using information from their assigned reading, problems, or video to inform their thinking.

How This FACT Promotes Student Learning

Homework Card Sort provides an alternative and engaging way for students to focus on, extract, and process information obtained through reading text, solving problems, or watching a video assigned for homework. As students discuss their ideas in small groups and relate them to the information gained from their reading, problem-solving set, or video assignment, they have an opportunity to clarify and solidify their thinking, gain new information by listening to others during discussion, provide feedback to each other on their thinking, and identify concepts or ideas they do not fully understand. The interactive and nonjudgmental nature of this FACT makes it more engaging to students than the traditional practice of assigning questions or problems from a textbook or video to individually answer for homework and go over the next day in class (usually a boring habit of practice!). After an initial positive experience with this FACT, disengaged students may be more motivated to complete homework assignments in preparation for this activity.

How This FACT Informs Instruction

This FACT provides an opportunity for teachers to gather feedback on the effectiveness of a homework assignment in helping students obtain, understand, and use new information from text or video. Instead of writing answers to questions and problems that often merely involve parroting back the text, repeating the same procedure, or watching a video with little or no conceptual understanding, *Homework Card Sort* reveals how well students are able to make sense of and use the information from the assignment. Teachers can observe which concepts, procedures, or ideas are well understood and which ones need further emphasis during instruction. Peer or teacher feedback can be provided to students to guide their learning as they share their thinking during the sorting process. Reading informational text in mathematics can be especially challenging for some students. This FACT can also be used to determine difficulties some students may have with reading and understanding informational text.

Design and Administration

Prepare a set of cards with statements or pictures that reflect the text or video assignment. Assign the text reading, problems, or video for homework and encourage students to jot down any important information from the assignment that will help them use what they read, solved, or viewed for an activity the next day (if they have previously encountered this strategy, they will know what to expect). In small groups, students use the cards to discuss the previous day's assignment by sorting them into categories provided by the teacher and discussing the reasons for each card's placement. Categories can be sorted on the basis of major concepts or procedures in the assignment, or cards that involve statements can be sorted into "agree" or "disagree" categories. Encourage students to refer back to their notes on the information they gained from their assignment or the problems they solved to support their card placement. If students disagree or if they are stuck during the sorting process, provide time at the end for them to go back to the text or video to obtain the information that resolves their disagreement or fills in any gaps.

As students sort the cards, make note of areas of difficulty that need to be addressed in subsequent instruction. Figure 3.21 is an example of a *Homework Card Sort* used during an instructional sequence on multiplying polynomials. Algebra students were assigned a video to watch based on using algebra tiles to model the multiplication of binomials and trinomials. The *Homework Card Sort* was given the next day to formatively assess what students learned from the assignment. They sorted the cards into Agree or Disagree based on the information they obtained from watching the video.

Connection to Mathematics Standards

This FACT can be used to evaluate the effectiveness of a homework assignment that provides information related to mathematical key ideas, as well as to identify concepts students do or do not understand from an assigned reading, problem set, or video. Depending on the assignment, any of the mathematical practices can be used with this FACT.

General Implementation Attributes

Ease of Use: Medium   **Time Demand:** Medium
Cognitive Demand: Medium

Figure 3.21   Example of an Algebra *Homework Card Sort*

$(x + 3)(x + 5) = x^2 + 15$	$(x + 3)(x + 4) = x^2 + 7x + 12$
$(2x + 5)\,(3x^2 - 4x + 2) = (3x^2 - 4x + 2)$ $(2x + 5)$	$(3x + 4)\,(2x + 8) = 6x^2 + 24x + 8x + 32$
The product of a binomial and a trinomial can be represented as an area of a rectangle.	When multiplying two binomials, each binomial can represent a dimension of a square.

$(x + 4)(x + 2)$ can be represented as	$(x + 2)(3x + 4)$ can be represented as
$(3x^2 + 3x - 5)\,(x + 1)$ can be represented as 	$3x^3$	$3x^2$	$-5x$	 	$3x^2$	$3x$	-5		$(x + 2)(x + 4)$ can be represented as 	$2x$	$2x$	 	$4x$	8	

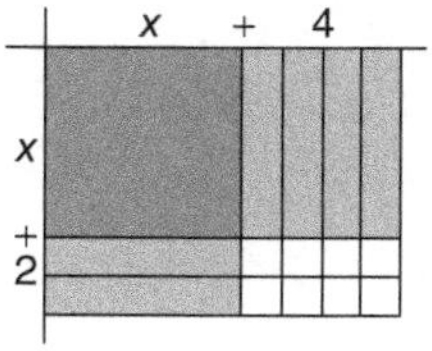

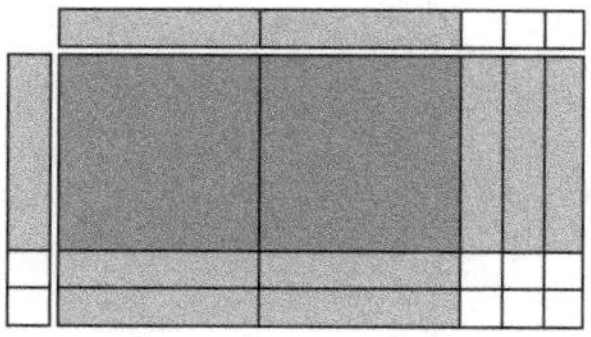

Modifications

This strategy can also be used with assignments that utilize websites. This strategy can be used with the flipped classroom. After students have viewed the video of the lesson or read an assigned text, the card sort can be used the next day to support their learning and provide formative assessment feedback used by the teacher.

Caveats

Do not prevent students who did not complete the homework assignment from participating in this FACT. This is a strategy that works particularly well with disengaged students who often fail to complete homework assignments. The act of sorting and discussing the cards appeals to and involves students in ways that worksheets or text and problems in the textbook do not. If some students did not complete the reading assignment, they should still participate with a group. Being part of the small group and listening to the discussion contributes to their learning, even if they did not do the required assignment, and may encourage them to complete the assignment the next time when they experience how this FACT is used.

Use With Other Disciplines

This FACT can also be used in science, social studies, language arts, health, foreign language, and performing arts. For example, in language arts it can be used with fiction to sort descriptions of characters or events in a story, according to categories identified by the teacher.

My Notes

_____

_____

_____

_____

_____

FACT 21

I THINK–I RETHINK

Description

I Think–I Rethink is a reflection FACT that can be used with mathematics journals and other mathematics notebook strategies. Students commit and record their initial thinking (I Think) in response to a mathematics question or probe. After students have had opportunities to explore, investigate, discuss, and learn about the concept or idea, they revisit their initial thinking and have an opportunity to revise it (I Rethink).

How This FACT Promotes Student Learning

I Think–I Rethink provides an opportunity for students to bring to the surface and think through their initial ideas. Revisiting their initial ideas, after they have had opportunities to learn the mathematics content, helps them realize that their initial ideas can be changed or refined when new information becomes available. As a reflection FACT, students can see how their own thinking has changed after they have had opportunities to learn more about the concept. It helps them become critical analysts of their own learning. This FACT also encourages students to use evidence from the data, examples, problems, and information recorded in their mathematics journals or notebooks to revise their initial ideas and write new mathematics explanations or solutions. This FACT mirrors the nature of mathematics, because mathematicians constantly conjecture and revise their thinking until the conjecture can be justified.

How This FACT Informs Instruction

I Think–I Rethink provides a record of student thinking before and after instruction. The initial *I Think* is used to gain insight into student understanding and inform opportunities to move their learning forward. The *I Rethink* provides insight into how students' ideas have changed as a result of their learning opportunities and whether additional instruction needs to be provided if students have not fully met the learning target. Feedback is provided by the teacher (and/or students) on their *I Think* and *I Rethink* pages.

Design and Administration

This FACT is used with journaling or other techniques where students keep a written, ongoing record of their work. It is used with investigative questions posed by the teacher or students—or with formative assessment probes that elicit students' initial ideas and lead into student mathematics investigations and activities designed to provide solutions or obtain new information. Students respond to the question in their notebooks with an initial *I Think* on the left side page of the notebook, dating the entry and leaving space on the page for feedback. The teacher can provide initial feedback on their initial entry that is then considered by the student as the class experiences a lesson or sequence of lessons designed to address the question posed (or students can exchange their notebooks and provide peer feedback). This feedback may also support their later revision by encouraging clarification of procedures or terminology, examples, details, need for additional evidence, and so on that will guide their learning experiences and will be used for the *I Rethink*.

After students record their initial *I Think*, they leave the right side of the page empty for the *I Rethink* that will come later and continue recording data, solutions, information, and other records of their learning on the other pages of their notebook. After students have completed lessons designed to address the question, as well as considering the feedback provided, they revisit their initial entry. On the facing page they date their *I Rethink* and use the data, solutions, and information recorded in their notebook from their lessons to revise their initial entry. They may change their initial explanation or elaborate on their initial entry by including new or more specific information and procedures, including evidence from examples recorded in their notebooks. Students are encouraged to cite the page(s) in their notebook they used to revise their initial entry. The teacher examines the *I Rethink* entry for evidence of meeting the learning target and may provide additional feedback.

For example, students might be asked whether $\frac{7}{8}$ divided by $\frac{1}{4}$ is less than or more than 1. In the *I Think*, students record their claim and describe their initial thinking to support their claim. Some students might exhibit a common misconception—based on the overgeneralization that "division always makes smaller"—that the answer will be less than 1. They might provide whole number examples to support their claim. At this point, the teacher might check students' notebooks and leave feedback, such as "Is this always true for all numbers? How might you find out if this is always true?" The students will consider this feedback during next steps in instruction. Or the teacher might use the formative assessment information to design and set up a series of stations for them to investigate the results of dividing various fractions and whole numbers using various concrete models and computer applications. The students eventually realize that whether the result is more or less than 1 depends on whether the dividend is larger or smaller than the divisor. Data from their mathematics investigations as well as information from class discussions that help them understand division with fractions are recorded in their notebooks. The students then go back to their *I Think* and consider how their claim changed or was strengthened and whether they should revise or refine their explanation. They then write their *I Rethink* on the adjoining page with their new claim, evidence, and reasoning and cite pages in their notebook where examples and information support their revised or refined thinking.

Connection to Mathematics Standards

This FACT can be used to formatively assess students' understanding of any of the key mathematical ideas. It can be used with all the mathematical practices. It is especially useful in critiquing a student's initial reasoning.

General Implementation Attributes

Ease of Use: Medium   **Time Demand:** Medium
Cognitive Demand: Medium

Modifications

This FACT can be used with the formative assessment probes in the *Uncovering Student Thinking* series (see the Appendix) or formative assessment probes developed by the teacher. Print copies of the probe on both sides of paper. Students date and complete the first side with their initial thinking. After students have had opportunities to learn about the idea(s), they can revisit the probe and use the opposite side to revise or extend their thinking, drawing upon the examples and information in their notebooks.

This FACT can be modified to an *I Think–I Rethink–We Now Think*. When using mathematics notebooks, another page or blank space can be added after the *I Rethink* space. After students complete the *I Rethink*, their work can be used during a whole-class discussion where students have an opportunity to share their revised thinking, evaluate each other's ideas, and come to a class agreement on the best answer or explanation. They can then complete a *We Now Think* based on the class consensus that is a further revision or refinement of their *I Rethink* explanation.

Caveats

Make sure feedback is specific enough to help students think further about the concept, procedure, or information they need to collect and record in their notebooks, or things they might include when they write their *I Rethink*. However, the feedback should not provide the answer or information to students, but it should guide them as they seek understanding.

Use With Other Disciplines

This FACT can also be used in science or social studies where students collect data and information to support their initial and revised thinking. For example, in science students may make a prediction about a phenomenon and explain the reason for their prediction. They can then test their prediction by making observations, record the data from their observations, and revise their initial claim and explanation based on the evidence from data recorded in their notebook.

My Notes

_____

_____

_____

_____

_____

FACT 22

INTERACTIVE WHOLE-CLASS CARD SORTING

Description

Interactive Whole-Class Card Sorting is a whole-group follow-up strategy to using *Card Sorts* (Keeley & Tobey, 2011). After students sort cards in pairs or in small groups, the teachers asks for volunteers or uses a random pick method such as *Popsicle Sticks* (Keeley & Tobey, 2011) to have a student select a card from their sort, designate the category it was placed in, and explain the reason for placing it in that category. The class continues to place cards in categories until all are sorted. If a student chooses to move a card from one category to another, he or she must present to the class why he or she thinks the card should be moved.

How This FACT Promotes Student Learning

Interactive Whole-Class Card Sorting provides an opportunity for students to activate their thinking as they access their prior knowledge, review material they learned, or apply their learning to new examples. As the class progresses through the cards, individual thinking may change as students' revisit examples and listen to the reasoning of their classmates. As students share how they initially sorted their cards, they put forth their own ideas for others to consider, strengthen their skills of explaining and justifying their thinking, evaluate the ideas of others, and modify their own thinking as new information convinces them to reconsider their original sort. *Interactive Whole-Class Card Sorting* can also be used to help students revisit material they learned previously to scaffold their learning for the next lesson.

How This FACT Informs Instruction

Interactive Whole-Class Card Sorting provides a way for the teacher to elicit students' preconceptions, assess students' ability to transfer knowledge when provided with new examples or contexts, and look for areas of uncertainty or disagreement among students that may signify the need for further instructional opportunities. The teacher is listening to students as they agree, disagree, or express their uncertainty allowing the teacher to observe how students' ideas are changing through discussion. The teacher notes examples that students may not agree on or sort incorrectly to address in subsequent lessons or during class discussion. It also provides an opportunity to gauge where the students are in their thinking after they have completed a card sort in pairs or small groups.

Design and Administration

Prepare sets of cards that align with the content goal of the lesson or cluster of lessons students will encounter. Provide students with category headers under which to sort their cards. Begin this FACT by having pairs or small groups of students complete the card sort. Encourage students to place the cards in a row or column under the category header rather than on top of each other so you can see how students sort each individual item. Have students work in small groups to discuss each card and come to a common agreement on which category to place it in. After pairs or small groups have sorted, begin the *Interactive Whole-Class Card Sorting* process by having a student select one of the cards and explain why he or she placed the card in a given category. On a class chart, record the example under the given category so that it is visible to the class as a record of the *Interactive Whole-Class Card Sorting*.

Continue having students take turns selecting a card from their initial sort until all the card examples have been placed on the class chart. If a student chooses to move an already placed card to a different category, have the student explain why he or she thinks the card should be moved.

For example, second-grade students work in groups of three to sort a set of eight cards into two categories: Triangles and Not Triangles. The cards include a right triangle, an equilateral triangle, a scalene triangle, and an upside-down triangle. Other cards include a figure with three rounded sides, a rectangle, a star-shaped figure made up of several triangles, and a three-sided figure that is not closed. After they sort their cards in small groups and discuss the reasons for their placement, the teacher has a larger set of cards made up that are the same as the students'. On the whiteboard, she draws two columns labeled Triangle and Not a Triangle. She asks a student to volunteer to pick a card from their sort and share where their group placed it: Eddie chooses the equilateral triangle and explains it is a triangle because it has three points. Another student adds that it has three sides. The class agrees that it should go under the Triangle category. The teacher uses a magnet to place the card under the Triangle category on the white board so that it is visible to the class.

Sofia goes next and chooses the triangle that has the single vertex pointed downward. She says it goes under the Not a Triangle. She explains that it is not a triangle because it is upside down and a single point needs to be at the top. Some students agree, and others disagree, stating that it is a triangle because it has three sides. The teacher leads a class discussion about whether the pointed parts of a triangle have to be in a certain direction.

Eventually the class comes to a consensus that the points can be in any orientation and it is a triangle as long as it has three sides and three points. The teacher makes a note to follow up with other examples later that show different orientations of the vertices of a triangle and decides to introduce the word *vertex* to help them describe the points of a triangle. The teacher places the card under the Triangle category and continues until all the cards have been discussed and recorded on the chart.

Connection to Mathematics Standards

This FACT can be used to formatively assess students' understanding of any of the key mathematical ideas. It also provides an opportunity to use the mathematics practices of attending to precision when communicating mathematically, reasoning abstractly and quantitatively, and constructing viable arguments and critiquing the reasoning of others as students share their reasons for their card placement.

General Implementation Attributes

Ease of Use: High   **Time Demand:** Medium   **Cognitive Demand:** Medium

Modifications

The FACT can be used with a Smartboard. If students completed the initial card sort in pairs, have students continue to interact in pairs for the whole-group card selection and discussion. Use fewer cards and more visuals with younger children.

Caveats

Make sure the examples and categories used for the cards are familiar to students.

Use With Other Disciplines

This FACT can also be used in science, social studies, language arts, foreign languages, health, and performing arts. For example, in social studies students might sort objects into things that were first invented by the ancient Chinese, to understand that many technologies modern society uses are based on technological achievements of ancient China.

My Notes

FACT 23

LEARNING INTENTIONS

Description

Learning Intentions are used to determine the goal for a lesson and make the purpose of that lesson explicit to students, so they know what they are expected to learn during a lesson. Sometimes called objectives, learning goals, or learning targets, the term *learning intention* is preferred by some advocates of feedback because of the emphasis on intentionality. The importance of *Learning Intentions* lies not in what you call them but in how you articulate them and then use them during your instruction (Creighton et al., 2015). *Learning Intentions* are shared with students, so they know what they are supposed to do and learn during the lesson. *Learning Intentions* are accompanied by *Success Indicators* (FACT 42). Both *Learning Intentions* and *Success Indicators* do the following:

- Give students a clear idea of what will be learned and why
- Transfer the responsibility for learning to the students (no teacher can do the learning for his or her students)
- Provide students with a way to monitor their own learning
- Help students focus on the purpose of the lesson and what they should be learning rather than merely on the completion of the activity
- Help teachers review progress and provide a clearer focus for instructional next steps
- Help break down broad standards or goals

How This FACT Promotes Student Learning

"Not all students have the same idea as their teachers about what they are meant to be doing in the classroom" (Wiliam, 2011, p. 52). Student engagement, motivation, and learning increase when students know what they are doing, why they are doing it, and if they are "getting it." Metacognition (being aware of your thinking and when you understand or do not understand) is an important component of formative assessment. Students who are self-regulated learners take responsibility for their own learning and consciously monitor how their learning is progressing. Providing students with a *Learning Intention* helps them focus on what it is they are expected to learn as opposed to the task they are to complete, because learning is not in the materials or tasks themselves but in the conceptual connections students are making as they manipulate materials or complete tasks. Thus, they become active participants in their learning rather than passive recipients (Heritage, 2010). Research has shown that students who are focused on the goals for a lesson have an increased motivation to learn (Ames, 1992) and "apply effort in acquiring new skills, seek to understand what is involved rather than just committing information to memory, persist in the face of difficulties and generally try to increase their competence" (Harlen, 2007, p. 65).

How This FACT Informs Instruction

The process of determining the *Learning Intention* for a lesson or series of lessons helps teachers focus on their goal for learning and ensures there is a strong match between the lesson and the intended learning. Once the *Learning Intention* is established, teachers can determine the *Success Indicators* (FACT 42) and select FACTs they will use to elicit the evidence that students are moving toward the goal for the lesson.

Design and Administration

In a standards-based system, first determine the state or national standard students will be expected to meet. Then think about the progression of learning that needs to take place for students to achieve that standard, matching the progression to the lesson or sequence of lessons planned (*Note:* A lesson can take place over more than one class period or day). For example, if a standard is a "big idea," think about the sub-ideas that students need to learn on their way to understanding that big idea. Each lesson should focus on the steps along the way and target an important idea or practice students need to understand and be able to use. That important idea or mathematical practice (or the two combined) is the *Learning Intention*. The *Success Indicators* (FACT 42) accompany the *Learning Intention* and describe what it takes to meet the *Learning Intention*, so they can be used as checkpoints along the way to monitor and self-assess progress. A *Learning Intention*

- should be specific to the lesson or sequence of lessons but align with an important key idea or practice in mathematics;
- should focus on conceptual understanding;
- should be written in language that is familiar to students;
- should be shared with students;
- should be referred to throughout a lesson and used as reflection at the end;

- should be used by both the teacher and student to maintain and focus the purpose for learning; and
- should align with the *Success Indicators.*

To understand how to best use *Learning Intentions* and *Success Indicators*, it is important to also understand how they should not be used. *Learning Intentions* and *Success Indicators* are *NOT*

- simply a list of "I will understand" and "I can" statements;
- a unit level "big idea" or state or national standard that broadly encompasses several sub-ideas;
- the agenda (First we will . . . ; then, we will . . .);
- only for the teacher; and
- introduced only at the beginning of the lesson.

At the beginning of the lesson, the *Learning Intention* should be posted and communicated to students. It is important to make sure students understand the *Learning Intention* (and *Success Indicators*) prior to undertaking the mathematical investigation, activity, or task. The goal for the teacher is to make sure students understand what they are aiming for during the lesson and to use different FACTs during the lesson to gather evidence of students' progress toward meeting the *Learning Intention*. At different points throughout the lesson, refer students to the *Learning Intention* (and *Success Indicators*), and always revisit them at the end of the lesson.

Sentence starters for developing *Learning Intentions* include, but are not limited to, the following:

- Today we will learn to . . .
- The target for today's lesson is . . .
- Today we will work toward standard . . .
- Understand that . . .
- Understand why . . .
- Understand what . . .
- Understand how . . .
- Relate ___ and ___ (i.e., understand the relationship)
- Distinguish between ___ and ___ (i.e., understand the difference between)
- Be able to use . . .

The following are grade-span examples of *Learning Intentions* for a specific lesson planned by a teacher within that grade span to address sub-ideas related to the big idea of measurement:

- **Grades K–2:** Understand length as a measure of how long something is.
- **Grades 3–5:** Understand why measurements with larger units can be rewritten using smaller units.
- **Grades 6–8:** Understand why the volume is of a right cylinder can be found using the formula $V = \pi r^2 h$.
- **Grades 9–12:** Understand that a cross section of a solid is an intersection of a plane (two-dimensional) and a solid (three-dimensional).

See the Appendix for resources on developing *Learning Intentions* and *Success Criteria*.

Connection to Mathematics Standards

This FACT can be used to establish lesson goals that include any of the mathematical key ideas and practices. Often a *Learning Intention* combines a key idea and practice. Pay close attention to the performance verbs used in your standards. With standards that are written more procedurally, ask, "What will my students understand if they are able to do _____?"

General Implementation Attributes

Ease of Use: High   **Time Demand:** Medium
Cognitive Demand: Depends on how the *Learning Intention* is written

Modifications

A *Learning Intention* is not fixed for a lesson and can change during the implementation of a lesson, based on difficulties students are having or finding out that a lesson isn't accomplishing what it was intended to do. Be aware that you may need to modify a *Learning Intention* even after it is shared with students.

Caveats

Avoid the token use of *Learning Intentions*. Many districts mandate posting the learning objective. Often, the teacher writes the objective on the board and points it out to students, who then copy it into their notebooks. However, it is never brought up again throughout or at the end of the lesson, resulting in a formulaic way of sharing the lesson objective, which Dylan Wiliam (2011) describes as the "wallpaper objective" (p. 56).

Make sure when developing *Learning Intentions* that you focus on the idea or concept, not the activity. For example, the K–2 *Learning Intention* "Understand length as a measure of how long something is" focuses on length as an idea. This is different from "Understand how to use paper-clips to measure the length of an object." In this latter example, the activity is emphasized rather than the bigger, generalizable idea that can be used for other units of measure.

Be aware that some districts discourage the use of "Understand" because it is not measurable. The purpose of a *Learning Intention* is to define what mathematics concept students will understand by the end of a lesson, so the purpose of the lesson is clear to students whereas the *Success Indicators* define what the students will be able to do and therefore need to be measureable. *Learning Intentions* and *Success Indicators* are intended to be used formatively rather than as a summative measurement of learning.

Use With Other Disciplines

This FACT can also be used in science, social studies, language arts, health, foreign language, and performing arts. For example, in an ELA class a *Learning Intention* might be "Understand that temporal words and phrases can be used to signal event order."

My Notes

_____

_____

_____

_____

_____

FACT 24

LEARNING INTENTIONS REFLECTION

Description

Learning Intentions Reflection is a set of questions used for reflection that relate to the identified *Learning Intentions* in a unit of instruction. Students are asked to reflect on the extent to which they feel they understand the mathematics in each *Learning Intention*.

How This FACT Promotes Student Learning

A key principle of assessment *for* learning is that students must know what the learning target is. Explicitly sharing *Learning Intentions* with students raises their awareness of the focus of a lesson. The *Learning Intentions Reflection* activates student thinking about a cluster of *Learning Intentions* that were addressed across a unit of study. It requires them to think about what they know in relation to the *Learning Intentions* as well as when and how they learned the mathematics.

How This FACT Informs Instruction

The *Learning Intentions Reflection* provides information to teachers on students' perceptions of their existing knowledge in relation to identified learning goals and the extent to which they learned the mathematical content. It also provides information on when and how students may have learned the mathematical ideas related to the learning goal. It provides an opportunity for teachers to determine whether he or she needs to differentiate instruction to meet the needs of students' prior to administering a summative assessment such as a quiz, mid-unit, or unit exam.

Design and Administration

Prior to the unit of instruction, identify the *Learning Intentions* and *Success Indicators* from the instructional materials or the state or national standards targeted in the unit of instruction. Create a question inventory for each *Learning Intention* in a set of lessons, such as the one shown in Figure 3.22 for a middle school unit on ratios. The first reflection date can be used at the beginning or partway through a sequence of instruction to determine prior and developing knowledge. It is revisited again after completing instruction on a set of *Learning Intentions* to determine whether students are ready to be summatively assessed or move on to the next set

Figure 3.22 *Learning Intentions Reflection* for a Set of Lessons on Ratios

Learning Intention	Reflection Date: _____	Reflection Date: _____
Understand that a ratio uses two numbers to describe a relationship between two things.	☐ I understand this fully. ☐ I am not there yet. Because:	☐ I understand this fully. ☐ I am not there yet. Because:
Know that while a fraction describes part of a whole, a ratio can describe a part-to-part relationship *or* a part-to-whole relationship.	☐ I understand this fully. ☐ I am not there yet. Because:	☐ I understand this fully. ☐ I am not there yet. Because:
Understand that ratios are always multiplicative relationships.	☐ I understand this fully. ☐ I am not there yet. Because:	☐ I understand this fully. ☐ I am not there yet. Because:
Know that a rate is a ratio, usually stated to imply that the two quantities can change.	☐ I understand this fully. ☐ I am not there yet. Because:	☐ I understand this fully. ☐ I am not there yet. Because:
Know that a unit rate is a rate stated so that one number in the ratio is 1.	☐ I understand this fully. ☐ I am not there yet. Because:	☐ I understand this fully. ☐ I am not there yet. Because:
Understand how unit rates can be used to compare different rates because they are both stated using 1 for a common quantity.	☐ I understand this fully. ☐ I am not there yet. Because:	☐ I understand this fully. ☐ I am not there yet. Because:

Source: Adapted from Example Unit Progression for Ratios and Rates Unit in Creighton, S. J., Tobey, C. R., Karnowski, E., & Fagan, E. (2015). *Bringing math students into the formative assessment equation: Tools and strategies for the middle grades.* Thousand Oaks, CA: Corwin.

A copy of this template can be downloaded at www.uncoveringstudentideas.org/templates.

of *Learning Intentions*. If they check off "I understand this fully," have them describe the "Because" in terms of how and when they learned the mathematics idea. If they check off "I am not there yet," have them describe the "Because" in terms of what they think they need to meet the *Learning Intention*. A template for this FACT is available at www .uncoveringstudentideas.org/templates.

Connection to Mathematics Standards

This FACT can be used to have students reflect on their learning related to any of the key ideas in mathematics. Since key ideas and mathematical practices are often combined in a *Learning Intention*, this FACT can support any of the mathematical practices.

General Implementation Attributes

Ease of Use: Medium   **Time Demand:** Medium
Cognitive Demand: Medium

Modifications

The *Learning Intentions Reflection* can be used in an oral discussion format with younger students or completed as a class anchor, posting several examples of students thinking or work that demonstrates understanding of each *Learning Intention*.

Caveats

Learning goals in state and national standards are interpreted in a variety of ways by teachers. Likewise, expect the same variation in interpretation from students. How one student may interpret a *Learning Intention* may be very different from how another student interprets it so it is important to refer to the *Learning Intentions* throughout instruction, therefore building a shared common understanding. By doing so, students will be better able to reflect on their own progress toward meeting the *Learning Intention*.

Use With Other Disciplines

This FACT can also be used in science, social studies, language arts, health, foreign languages, and visual and performing arts. For example, before beginning a series of lessons on physical and chemical changes, a middle school science teacher might have students complete the first column to reflect back on what they learned during a previous grade, which will help the teacher plan for subsequent instruction. The teacher has students reflect again after completing a set of lessons in which the *Learning Intentions* were addressed to determine the extent to which instruction was successful and whether students are ready to move on to the next set of lessons or assessment.

My Notes

_____

_____

_____

_____

_____

FACT 25

LET'S KEEP THINKING

Description

Let's Keep Thinking is used to encourage students to revisit their initial ideas and keep thinking throughout a lesson or a sequence of lessons. Instead of immediately giving students the answer after using a formative assessment probe or other FACT that elicits students' initial ideas, this FACT signals to the students that their ideas may change and that they should keep monitoring their thinking throughout a sequence of learning.

How This FACT Promotes Student Learning

Let's Keep Thinking encourages metacognition—that is, students' awareness of their own learning and thought processes—and the awareness that students' thinking may change as they develop mathematical ideas. Combined with other FACTs, it helps students accept that their initial ideas may not be the best ideas mathematically and that they, as well as the class as a whole, will persevere, continuing to develop and refine their mathematical knowledge and understanding. When students are given the answer after they have been presented with a question or are asked to commit to an outcome, they no longer think about it. The thinking ends when the teacher gives the answer. This FACT lets students hang out in uncertainty for a while, thus creating a desire to find out. By grappling with, thinking through, and discovering the answer or outcome themselves rather than being given the answer or outcome by the teacher, learning is strengthened and more likely to stay with the student rather than be forgotten.

How This FACT Informs Instruction

Let's Keep Thinking provides an opportunity for students to revisit and revise their ideas, because they are provided with opportunities to gather evidence and new information that may change their initial thinking. The FACT allows teachers to monitor how students' ideas are changing, make instructional decisions targeting ideas that are resistant to change, and differentiate for students who have difficulty moving toward the mathematically acceptable idea.

Design and Administration

This FACT can be used with assessment probes or other elicitation activities in which students may express a variety of different ideas.

The first step in using this FACT is to record students' initial thinking. FACTs such as *Sticky Bars* (Keeley & Tobey, 2011), *Extended Sticky Bars* (FACT 8), *VDR* (*Vote, Discuss, Revote*) (FACT 48), *Group Frayer Model* (FACT 18), or a chart of class ideas from *Conjecture Cards* (FACT 4) provide a class record of initial ideas. The teacher can also make a list of students' ideas on chart paper and post the list in the classroom. Above the class record of ideas, the teacher posts a sign or writes, "Let's Keep Thinking!" That is a signal that the probe or question will be revisited and new ideas will be compared with the class' initial ideas. As new ideas are generated or prior ideas are changed, the teacher refers to the initial record of class ideas and engages the students in a discussion of what changed their thinking and which ideas they now consider to be their best thinking. The *Let's Keep Thinking* chart stays posted and is referred to until the class can come to a consensus as to the best answer or explanation.

For example, a teacher may ask students to consider two jars of marbles. One jar has three blue marbles and two red marbles. The other jar has six blue marbles and four red marbles. Students are asked to predict whether the chance of getting a blue marble is better in the first jar, second jar, or is the chance the same. Five students predicted there would be a better chance of drawing a blue marble in the first jar. Nine students predicted there would be a better chance in the second jar, and six students thought there would be an equal chance in each jar. As students discussed the problem, the teacher made a list of class ideas about probability. She noticed some students focused on absolute size while others used doubling, ratios, and percentages to describe the outcome. Some students chose the correct answer, but in their explanations they said you can never know for sure because anything can happen.

The students wanted to know the answer to the problem. The teacher explained that they would be doing several activities after which they would revisit the probe and have an opportunity to change their thinking. She reminded them to keep thinking throughout the activities they will do next about how their thinking about chance might be changing. She put a "Let's Keep Thinking" sign above the class set of ideas.

She then planned several activities for students and revisited the probe again a few days later. This time all but two students predicted there would be an equal chance of getting a blue marble from either jar. After a class discussion and a revision of the chart of class ideas, the teacher checked with the two students who had not changed their initial ideas and found that the class discussion now changed their thinking and that they were able to show that both jars had a probability of 3 out of 5.

Connection to Mathematics Standards

This FACT can be used to formatively assess students' understanding of any of the key mathematical ideas and practices. It is especially useful in constructing viable arguments and critiquing the reasoning of others because students must revisit and critique initial explanations and revise them as they apply new mathematical thinking.

General Implementation Attributes

Ease of Use: Medium   **Time Demand:** Medium
Cognitive Demand: Medium

Modifications

Let's Keep Thinking can be used with students' mathematical drawings and other conceptual models of their thinking. Students post their drawings under a *Let's Keep Thinking* sign. When their conceptual models change, students may revise their drawing or replace it with a new one.

Caveats

It is important to refrain from clueing students or acknowledging students who are correct. The goal is for all students to keep thinking, even students who have a correct understanding benefit from solidifying their ideas and using them to engage in argumentation.

Use With Other Disciplines

This FACT can also be used in science, social studies, language arts, and health. For example, in science students can post their initial answers to a probe using the *Extended Sticky Bars*. As they gain more information and evidence and engage in scientific and sense-making discussions, they may revise their original answer and explanation.

My Notes

_____

_____

_____

_____

_____

FACT 26

LINES OF AGREEMENT

Description

Lines of Agreement is used in situations where students are asked to agree or disagree with a statement or viewpoint. The FACT can be used to uncover students' preconceptions prior to instruction or elicit evidence of the extent to which they can use the mathematics they have been learning to support an argument. Students face each other in opposite lines, representing their mathematical statement or answer choice, and then engage in argumentation to explicate and defend their reasoning. If at any time an argument from one side is compelling enough for a student to change his or her thinking, he or she may cross over to the other line.

How This FACT Promotes Student Learning

Lines of Agreement activates students' thinking, since they have to commit to a mathematical statement or claim and be prepared to support it. The practice of mathematical argumentation is strengthened because students use the mathematics and apply their mathematical reasoning skills to support their ideas. As students present and defend their arguments, they also ask questions of each other and learn to respectfully challenge and critique an argument. Responding to the questions and challenges of other students helps students think more deeply about their own ideas and the mathematics they used to support their ideas. Students who do not speak and offer an argument during this FACT are still learning through the act of listening to and evaluating the arguments of others and crossing over to the other line if others' arguments change their thinking.

How This FACT Informs Instruction

By listening to students as they engage in mathematical arguments, the teacher becomes aware of the extent to which students can use mathematics concepts and terminology accurately, support their claims with sufficient and appropriate evidence, use mathematical and logical reasoning, listen attentively, and follow norms for productive mathematics talk. The teacher can also note the extent to which students are able to engage in mathematical argumentation using proof and justification, as distinguished from the type of arguments that are used in an everyday context or in other disciplines that involve different norms and types of evidence for debate.

Design and Administration

Choose a question with two different choices (yes, no; true, false; one attribute or another) that can be used for opposite views on a topic or concept. For example, a class of high school students can be presented with the following question: Is this pattern exponential or quadratic? Students form two facing lines—those who think it is exponential and those who think that it is quadratic.

Give students time to think and commit to a claim. Use a quiet, individual quick write to encourage students to write down their initial ideas and explain their thinking. When the class is ready, have them form two lines, facing each other, that represent their opposing claims. The teacher's role is to facilitate the argumentation session. Using norms, such as that only one person at a time may speak, provide opportunities for students on both sides to present their arguments, rebuttals, and to question each other. Occasionally, you may need to toss in a question or redirect the arguments of students who are veering from the topic. After a compelling argument or rebuttal, ask if any students wish to cross over to the other side based on what they heard so far. Note how and which students are changing their thinking and what evidence was presented in the argument that led students to change their ideas and cross over to the other side. If an argument was valid, you might expand on it after the session, discussing the quality of the evidence and justification. If students changed their thinking based on an invalid argument, consider how to address this during follow-up instruction, but do not correct it during the argumentation session.

The goal is to allow the students the opportunity to present their arguments and make their thinking public. It is important to facilitate and listen to students but not correct students or offer your own explanations during the argumentation session. Later, the teacher will use the information gathered from listening to both groups to design learning opportunities that will confront students with their ideas and help them refine or revise their claims and arguments as they consider the mathematics needed to support a claim. For example, as students argue about whether a decimal is or is not a type of fraction, the teacher listens carefully and notes the characteristics students use to determine whether something is a fraction. The teacher can also use this FACT to provide feedback on how well the students use the practice of engaging in mathematical argumentation and what they can do to improve their arguments. If used as elicitation, the FACT uncovers preexisting ideas. If used after a concept has been taught, the FACT uncovers the extent to which students are able to apply and use the concept.

Connection to Mathematics Standards

This FACT can be used to formatively assess students' understanding of any of the mathematical key ideas. It is used to support the practice of constructing viable arguments and critiquing the reasoning of others. It supports the construction of explanations used during an argument when conflicting conjectures are presented.

General Implementation Attributes

Ease of Use: Medium   **Time Demand:** Medium
Cognitive Demand: Medium

Modifications

This strategy can be used with the *Opposing Views Probes* FACT (Keeley & Tobey, 2011). Students may be asked to turn and talk to a partner standing next to them before starting the session so they have an opportunity to first practice explaining their thinking and getting feedback from a partner to strengthen their argument. To avoid "ping-pong"—back-and-forth arguments between the same students—you might enact a speaking rule such as two or three before me, in which two or three other students must speak until the first student can speak again.

Caveats

This strategy should be used only after students have had an opportunity to learn about what constitutes a mathematics argument and have developed agreed upon norms for respectful and productive mathematics talk. Be careful not to correct students, explain, or coach students as they engage in argumentation because the ideas should come from the students, not the teacher (the teacher addresses students' ideas as part of subsequent instruction). Make sure all students have equal opportunities to speak and listen and that no one is allowed to dominate the discussion.

Use With Other Disciplines

This FACT can also be used in science, social studies, language arts, and health, where students are involved in debate, argument, proof, or justification. For example, in social studies students debate whether there should be term limits in Congress. One side is in favor of term limits; one side is not in favor of term limits.

My Notes

_____

_____

_____

_____

_____

FACT 27

MOST AND LEAST SURE ABOUT

Description

In this self-assessment technique, students are asked to identify two or four items from a problem set—one or two they are most sure about regarding solving correctly and one or two they are least sure about. The information is used as feedback to the teacher to identify problem areas.

How This FACT Promotes Student Learning

Most and Least Sure About promotes metacognition and helps students develop self-assessment skills because they think about which problems they could solve easily and which ones were more difficult for them. The strategy supports students as owners of their own learning.

How This FACT Informs Instruction

This FACT provides an opportunity for teachers to gather information on how students feel they are progressing on independent practice items assigned during class or as homework. Using this quick check-in, class patterns are easily visible and help the teacher determine next instructional steps. For example, if there is an equal number of votes for an item in the *Most Sure About* group as the *Least Sure About* group, pairing students is a viable responsive action. If the majority of votes in the *Least Sure About* group are for the same item, additional whole-group instruction is an appropriate next step.

Design and Administration

Provide each student with two to four small sticky notes. Ask students to write the number of the item(s) they are most sure about and least sure about, labeling each note with Most and Least. Gather the sticky notes and display them so students can see the class responses or have the students place their sticky notes on a class chart with two columns: *Problems We Are Most Sure About* and *Problems We Are Least Sure About*. Move sticky notes around to form groups of the same items. For example, after completing a set of problems where students find the area of a space inside a figure by tiling, the teacher can have students select two problems they are most sure about getting the correct answer and two problems they are less sure about getting the correct answer. Depending on the patterns of items in each category, choose a responsive action such as the following:

- If same problem appears in both categories, create groups of students so that there is at least one student in the group who had the item in the Most Sure About category.
- If the majority of the items in the Most Sure About category are similar, choose one to two students to explain their process and ask the other students to compare their approach the presented approach.
- If the majority of the items in the Least Sure About category are similar, elicit additional evidence to determine whether to provide additional instruction or feedback.

Connection to Mathematics Standards

This FACT can be used to formatively assess students' understanding of mathematical key ideas used in problem solving. This FACT supports the mathematical practice of making sense of problems and persevering in solving them.

General Implementation Attributes

Ease of Use: High   **Time Demand:** Medium   **Cognitive Demand:** Medium

Modifications

Data can be collected and displayed using personal response system (clickers) or apps for data display. *Most and Least Sure About* can also be used after pair or group work on an item set. This strategy can also be used to review practice test items to determine what types of items students have the most success or difficulty with before they take a test.

Caveats

It is important for students to be learning resources for each other. However, when pairing students for intervention, make sure the Most Sure About students who are matched up to help the Least Sure About students have an accurate grasp of the content or skill targeted by the lesson so that one student's misunderstandings will not be passed on to another. Choose students carefully for peer assistance and, if possible, listen in on the discussions to determine how well students are able to assist others.

Use With Other Disciplines

This FACT can also be used in science, social studies, language arts, health, foreign languages, and visual and performing arts. For example, a chemistry teacher might use this strategy to review a homework assignment on stoichiometry problems.

My Notes

_____

_____

_____

_____

_____

FACT 28

NOW ASK ME A QUESTION

Description

Now Ask Me a Question is a technique that switches roles from the teacher as the generator of questions to the student as the question generator. Asking good questions does not come naturally for many students. The ability to formulate good questions about a mathematical topic can indicate the extent to which a student understands ideas that underlie the topic. This FACT provides a structured method for students to generate questions in pairs.

How This FACT Promotes Student Learning

Students typically think that asking questions is easy and answering them is difficult (Naylor, Keogh, & Goldsworthy, 2004, p. 120). When they are put in a position to develop thinking questions that go beyond recall, they realize they have to draw on their own understanding of the topic. Generating good questions in mathematics requires more than superficial knowledge of the topic. It requires students to delve deeper into their existing knowledge base. As they formulate "thinking questions," they practice metacognition by recognizing the level of understanding needed not only to form the question but to respond to it as well.

How This FACT Informs Instruction

The numbers of questions students come up with, the quality of the questions (recall versus thinking questions), and the sophistication of the ideas embedded in the question reveal information about students' knowledge. As students learn to distinguish productive questions from nonproductive ones, their higher level questions reveal interesting insights into their thinking about the mathematics content. Teachers can also have students exchange or answer their own questions, revealing further information about students' ideas related to the mathematics topic.

Design and Administration

After a presentation, by the teacher or a student, instead of asking questions this way:

Are there any questions?

Do you have any questions?

You don't have any questions, do you?

Would anyone like to see that again?

Instead, say, "Now, ask me a question." Have the students work in pairs to develop a question about the content that was just presented. To help students develop good questions, the teacher can provide a list of question stems or post a chart of question stems to refer to in the classroom.

The following are samples of question-generating stems for mathematics:

- Why does _____?
- Does anyone have a different way to explain _____?
- How can you prove _____?
- Is _____ always true?
- What would happen if _____?
- What is the difference between _____ and _____?
- How can you solve for _____?
- What rule explains _____?
- What would happen to the pattern if _____?
- What is a different way to represent _____?
- How could we find out if _____?
- What math facts support _____?
- Does _____ when _____?
- How does _____ relate to _____?
- How are _____ and _____ related?
- What effect does _____ have on _____?
- What is the significance of _____?
- How many different ways can you _____?
- Why did you do _____ before _____?
- How can you make a model to show that?
- What is another method that would work?
- Is there a more efficient strategy?
- How would this work with other numbers?
- What if you had started with _____ rather than _____?
- What if you could only use _____?
- What would a counterexample be?

For example, after completing a set of activities on parallelograms, middle school students might ask:

- If there are two right angles, will a four-sided figure always be a parallelogram?
- How many different ways can you draw a parallelogram?
- How are rhombuses and parallelograms related?
- What rules apply to all parallelograms?
- What has to be true about opposite angles and parallelograms?

Connection to Mathematics Standards

This FACT can be used to formatively assess students' understanding of any mathematical key ideas. It also provides an opportunity to develop questions that promote the use of any of the mathematical practices.

General Implementation Attributes

Ease of Use: Medium   **Time Demand:** Medium
Cognitive Demand: High for higher level questions

Modifications

Questions can be developed individually and followed by having students work in groups of three to four to respond to each question. Those questions the group has difficulty answering can be shared during whole-class follow-up.

Caveats

Some students, particularly younger students, may lack the prior knowledge to answer some *how* or *why* questions. These questions could be better phrased with stems such as "Why do you think . . ." rather than "Why does . . ."

Use With Other Disciplines

This FACT can also be used in science, social studies, language arts, health, foreign languages, and visual and performing arts. For example, in science a set of questions can be developed on the topic of plate tectonics after students have watched a video of a scientist explaining where Earth's plates are found and the interactions between plates.

My Notes

FACT 29

PARTNER STRATEGY ROUNDS

Description

Partner Strategy Rounds provides an opportunity for students to examine others' strategies, compare them to their own, and then practice posing and responding to questions about their work.

How This FACT Promotes Student Learning

This FACT involves examining the strategies others use to solve mathematical problems. As students engage in this FACT, they build on others' strategies or add new strategies of their own. "Thinking cannot be articulated unless students reflect on the problem and the strategies used to solve it; articulation, in turn, increases reflection, which leads to understanding" (Fennema & Romberg, 1999, p. 188). Often in whole-group sharing situations, not all students have a chance to share, ask, and respond to questions due to either time constraints or comfort level. This FACT provides an opportunity for all students to share their strategies, ask questions of others, and respond to others' questions. As students reflect on the questions and responses, they may self-correct or obtain new strategies for solving problems.

How This FACT Informs Instruction

Partner Strategy Rounds elicit different processes students use to solve a problem. As students are sharing, the teacher can gather information on the range of strategies used to determine those to be shared with the whole class. Used prior to instruction, *Partner Strategy Rounds* enable the teacher to use the information to plan lessons that move students toward a particular strategy or process. Used during or after the concept development stage, teachers can use the FACT to gather information to determine students' ability to apply a strategy within a problem context.

Design and Administration

Prior to using this FACT, use a recording sheet template such as the one in Figure 3.23 (this template can be downloaded from www.uncoveringstudentideas.org/templates). Allow students time to individually complete the problem, using the first section of the recording sheet to record their processes and solutions. Determine the amount of time and number of partner rounds based on the complexity of the problem. Start by asking the students to find a Round 1 partner. Each pair chooses who

| Figure 3.23 | Example *Partner Questioning Rounds* Recording Sheet |

My work:

Round 1	
Question for my partner:	My partner's question for me:
Reflection on my partner's answer:	Reflection on my answer:

Round 2	
Question for my partner:	My partner's question for me:
Reflection on my partner's answer:	Reflection on my answer:

Round 3	
Question for my partner:	My partner's question for me:
Reflection on my partner's answer:	Reflection on my answer:

A copy of this template can be downloaded at www.uncoveringstudentideas.org/templates.

will be Partner 1 and who will be Partner 2. Partner 1 then explains his or her strategy while Partner 2 asks a question using selected question stems posted by the teacher (see FACT 28 for examples of question stems), after Partner 1 answers the question, a quick reflection on the answer is recorded, and then the roles are reversed. Continue the process with two to three additional partners. At the end of the *Partner Questioning Rounds*, ask for a few volunteers to share a question and response that were discussed during their round.

For example, algebra students might be given a complex problem that involves use of order of operations with all four operations, exponents, and parentheses. Each student works out the problem individually before meeting in pairs. One student asks, "Why did you do the multiplication before the division?" This caused the student to reflect back on what she learned about PEMDAS and realized that multiplication and division are taken together and performed according to which is first rather than thinking multiplication must be done before division.

Connection to Mathematics Standards

This FACT can be used to formatively assess students' understanding mathematics key ideas used for problem solving. It is especially useful in providing an opportunity for students to use the practices of making sense of problems and persevering in solving them and attending to precision when communicating their solutions.

General Implementation Attributes

Ease of Use: Medium   **Time Demand:** Medium
Cognitive Demand: High (depends on problem)

Modifications

Students can work in pairs on a problem and form groups of four to share strategies. The time interval and number of partners can be changed to reflect the complexity of the problem. For less complex problems, a more random approach can be used, with students moving quickly from partner to partner to find strategies that differ from their own in at least one way.

Caveats

This strategy may be difficult for ELLs or students who have a hard time concentrating or hearing. There is a high level of noise in the classroom when many students are talking at the same time. Have them spread out so they may better hear their partners.

Use With Other Disciplines

This FACT can also be used in science or social studies to determine how other students solve an engineering or social problem.

My Notes

FACT 30

PLUS–DELTA

Description

Plus–Delta (+/Δ) is a feedback FACT used to identify what is working well for students during the learning process and what needs to be changed. The Greek letter delta, Δ, is the symbol used in mathematics and science to represent change.

How This FACT Promotes Student Learning

This FACT provides a metacognitive opportunity for students to think about their learning and take responsibility for providing feedback that the teacher can use to improve students' learning opportunities. *Plus–Delta* helps students focus on what works for them in advancing their learning (Plus) and what needs to be changed or improved to help them learn better (Delta).

How This FACT Informs Instruction

This FACT provides immediate feedback to the teacher on what strategies, techniques, or parts of a lesson positively impact students' learning (Plus) and what aspects of instruction need to be changed (Delta). Used at the end of a class period or a lesson, the teacher uses the feedback to plan for the next lesson or identify the need to differentiate for different groups of students in the class.

Design and Administration

Create a *Plus–Delta* wall chart. At the end of class, give each student two sticky notes and ask them to label them with a + and Δ. On the + note, have them write what helped them learn in today's lesson. On the Δ note, have them write what needs to be changed so that they can learn. Have students place their sticky notes on the chart, under the appropriate column, as you end the lesson. Alternatively, you can design a +/Δ exit slip, such as the one in Figure 3.24, which students fill out at the end of class and turn in as they leave the classroom, either anonymously or with their names on it (a downloadable copy of a +/Δ exit slip is available at www.uncoveringstudentideas.org/templates).

The responses are analyzed by the teacher, especially making note of ones that are similar among a significant number of students. This is a strong indication of what is working well for the class or what needs instructional attention. Look for indications where differentiation might

| Figure 3.24 | *Plus–Delta* Exit Slip |

＋ **This helped me learn**	Δ **This could be changed to help me learn**

A copy of this template can be downloaded at www.uncoveringstudentideas.org/templates.

be helpful for certain students. For example, students worked together in small groups to solve a thought experiment. The question asked, "If you could tie a string around the Earth so it rested on the surface of the Earth, then untied it, added six more meters of string, and pulled the string out equally away from the Earth in all directions, what would be the largest animal that could walk under the string? A sample of plus (+) feedback might be "This problem was really challenging. I liked that it was so different from typical problems we get about circumference. I like how we got to make a model using a basketball and string to test our idea. I could see how an animal much larger than what we predicted could go under the string once we made our model." The delta (Δ) might be "I'm still having a hard time understanding the proportional relationship using the equation that was on the board. I think I need more time to work through it and use it myself as it is hard to understand just watching someone solve it."

Connection to Mathematics Standards

This FACT can be used to formatively assess students' understanding of any of the mathematics key ideas. It can be used to give feedback on how any of the practices were used in instruction.

General Implementation Attributes

Ease of Use: High   **Time Demand:** Low   **Cognitive Demand:** Low

Modifications

This FACT can be modified as a self-reflection by having students reflect on what they are doing that is improving their own learning (Plus) and what changes they need to make to improve their learning (Delta). It can also be used to reflect on how well a group is working together by describing what the group is doing well to support each other's learning (Plus) and what the group needs to do better so everyone in the group is supported in their learning (Delta). The feedback can also be recorded by the teacher on the chart, as the students publicly share their pluses and deltas in an end-of-lesson debrief.

Caveats

Make sure students know how their feedback will be used. It is important to close the feedback loop with students, reporting back the data to them and how you plan to use it to improve your teaching and their learning.

Use With Other Disciplines

This FACT can also be used in science, social studies, language arts, health, foreign languages, and visual and performing arts. For example, in the performing arts, as students practice for a play, they may complete a *Plus–Delta* to describe what aspects of the practice help them prepare for their performance and what aspects of the practice needed to be changed to better prepare them for their performance.

My Notes

FACT 31

PMI (PLUS–MINUS–INTERESTING)

Description

Plus–Minus–Interesting (PMI) is a FACT that can be used when students present their mathematics arguments. It is modified from the "Father of Lateral Thinking," Edward de Bono's (1994) original *PMI* strategy for weighing the pros and cons of decisions. *PMI* provides a record of what the student was thinking as he or she evaluated the mathematics arguments shared by classmates.

How This FACT Promotes Student Learning

PMI is used to evaluate peers' mathematical arguments. Students often rush to judgment when presented with an argument. This FACT provides an opportunity for students to examine the quality of an argument before agreeing or disagreeing. As students use this FACT, they gain practice in identifying the strengths and weaknesses of their peers' arguments and note interesting ideas that may spark new questions, leading to further mathematical investigations and problem solving. *PMI*s can also be used for giving peer feedback on the quality of proof and justification, so students can improve their arguments. The *PMI* FACT encourages students to consider alternative explanations and can help the class reach consensus regarding a mathematics conjecture.

How This FACT Informs Instruction

"Mathematically proficient students understand and use stated assumptions, definitions, and previously established results in constructing arguments" (CCSSO, 2010). For their arguments to be valid and convincing, students' mathematical claims must be supported with appropriate and sufficient evidence. As students present their arguments to others, orally or through writing, students should be encouraged to evaluate the strengths or weaknesses of others' arguments. *PMI* provides a record of how students evaluate an argument. It provides a window for the teacher to examine whether students can critically analyze a mathematics argument. Results from this FACT may indicate the need to help students understand what constitutes appropriate and sufficient mathematics proof and evidence. It may also indicate a need to further develop students' reasoning skills so they can link proof and evidence to a claim. The third part of this FACT, *Interesting*, can be used as feedback for further investigation and discussion of mathematics ideas.

Design and Administration

Mathematical arguments take place informally, as students are collaboratively engaged in their work, and formally during class presentations. Arguments in mathematics are logical and compelling discussions that involve conjecture, evidence, justification, critical examination, revision, and refinement for the purpose of making a case, resolving questions, and seeking to understand. It is important that students not only develop mathematical arguments, but they also need to be able to critique the reasoning of others.

As individual students or small groups share their arguments, orally or in writing, these arguments are peer critiqued by recording the strengths of the argument (P or Plus), the flaws or weaknesses in the argument (M or Minus), and interesting things to note for further consideration that do not fit into either the P or the M category (I or Interesting) and may raise questions for further investigation. Their arguments may involve claims or solutions based on the conclusion of a mathematical investigation or the modeling of a contextual problem.

For example, students work in small groups to determine the best dimensions for packing a product. Students investigate how the size of the dimensions of the package relates to the amount of materials needed to make the package. They brainstorm and discuss a cost effective design for their package and then present their design to the class, with an argument about why they think their design will be the most cost effective. As they present arguments for their design, students note the strengths of their argument in supporting their design (P), weaknesses in their argument that do not support their design or something they overlooked (M), and other interesting parts of their argument that are neither strengths or weaknesses, including questions for further consideration (I). Students record the *PMIs* for each group's presentation and the teacher analyzes them, looking for evidence of understanding of the concept of volume and surface area and the extent to which students are able to critically evaluate an argument.

Students can be provided with an individual *PMI* recording sheet for each argument, or they may use a recording sheet similar to the one in Figure 3.25, to keep a class record of the *PMIs* for each argument (a downloadable copy of this template is available at www.uncoveringstudent ideas.org/templates). After a student, a pair, or a small group presents their argument, give students time to record their *PMIs*. They can also be encouraged to do this as they are listening to the arguments. *PMIs* can be collected and analyzed by the teacher to assess students' ability to evaluate an argument, or they can be shared in class to provide peer feedback for the purpose of improving arguments. They can also be used to come to a class consensus about the best argument(s).

Figure 3.25 *PMI* Template

PMI Class Record of Our Mathematics Arguments			
Student or Group	**Plus (Strengths of the argument)**	**Minus (Weaknesses of the argument)**	**Interesting (Including new questions for consideration)**

A copy of this template can be downloaded at www.uncoveringstudentideas.org/templates.

Connection to Mathematics Standards

This FACT can be used to formatively assess students' understanding of mathematics key ideas used in arguments. It especially provides an opportunity to formatively assess the practices of reasoning abstractly and quantitatively, modeling with mathematics, constructing viable arguments and analyzing the reasoning of others, and attending to precision.

General Implementation Attributes

Ease of Use: Medium   **Time Demand:** Medium
Cognitive Demand: Medium

Modifications

This FACT can be combined with the *Gallery Walk* (see FACT 17). Students can provide feedback directly on students' posters or charts that represent their ideas, investigations, or solutions using different colored sticky notes for P, M, and I. *PMI* can be practiced by providing students with a written or oral "canned argument" developed by the teacher for the purpose of introducing the FACT for the first time to students. The teacher-developed example gives students an opportunity to use a canned argument to practice giving appropriate and constructive *PMI* feedback.

Caveats

Before using this FACT, make sure students know how a mathematics argument differs from an everyday argument and ensure that students have developed and accepted norms and behaviors for engaging in productive mathematics talk and argument. Make sure students understand how to provide constructive feedback that can help others improve the quality and strength of their arguments.

Use With Other Disciplines

This FACT can also be used in science, social studies, language arts, and health. For example, students often debate issues in social studies. *PMI* can be used to give feedback on the strengths and weaknesses of the debaters' points and interesting points shared during the debate. It can also be used to view and evaluate an actual debate between two people (e.g., a presidential debate during an election year).

My Notes

FACT 32

QUESTIONING CUE CARDS

Description

Questioning Cue Cards provide a structured opportunity for students to examine others' processes and strategies, compare them to their own, and then practice posing and responding to questions about the work. While examining others' processes, students build on them or add new processes of their own.

How This FACT Promotes Student Learning

"Thinking cannot be articulated unless students reflect on the problem and the strategies used to solve it; articulation, in turn, increases reflection, which leads to understanding" (Fennema & Romberg, 1999, p. 188). The cue cards help students focus on others' thinking and problem-solving techniques. This analysis is then used to generate a question, supporting higher level thinking.

How This FACT Informs Instruction

Questioning Cue Cards elicit different strategies and processes students use to solve a problem. As students are sharing, the teacher can gather information on the range of strategies and processes used to determine those to be shared with the whole class. *Questioning Cue Cards* enables the teacher to use the information to plan next steps to move students toward a particular strategy or process.

Design and Administration

Prepare sets of *Questioning Cue Cards*, such as those shown in Figure 3.26, so that each group of four students has a set of cards, one for each student in their group. (A template for this FACT can be found at www.uncoveringstudentideas.org/templates.) It is preferable to create Card 1 using a different color than the other three cards. The holder of Card 1 is the student who presents his or her process and responds to the questions asked by the other students in the group. Use a random method to determine which student gets each card or ask for volunteers in the group to be first person with Card 1.

Display a problem to be solved and allow students time to individually complete the problem. When ready, prompt the student with Card 1 to share his or her thinking with the other students in the group. After the student with Card 1 shares, each group member asks or responds to the

| Figure 3.26 | Example *Questioning Cue Cards* |

1 I did/found/got _____ by/because _____ .	2 You said _____ . Why did you _____ ?
3 Can you tell me more about _____ ?	4 Can you show me another way to _____ ?

A copy of this template can be downloaded at www.uncoveringstudentideas.org/templates.

student using the question stem on his or her card (Cards 2, 3, or 4). Have at last four problems or prompts prepared to rotate the cards and give each student a chance to present their thinking and use each of the other prompt stems.

For example, third-grade students were working on problems with remainders. The teacher wanted to assess if they understand whether a remainder is rounded depends on the context of the problem. The problem they discussed was "Jason has 27 new baseball cards to add to his baseball card album. He can fit six baseball cards on a page. How many pages does he need to add all his new baseball cards?" Each student completes the problem individually and then discusses it in a small group using the *Questioning Cue Cards*.

The student with Card 1 says, "I got 3 whole pages and part of another page by dividing 27 by 6 and getting three cards left over." The student with Card 2 says, "You said you had three cards leftover. Why did you say you need part of a page rather than using another whole page?" The student replies, "Because there aren't enough cards for a whole page." Student 3 says, "Can you tell me more about how you were thinking about the remainder?" The student thinks about this and then says, "Well, at first I divided and got the remainder, but now that I think about it, three cards are the remainder, but this is about how many pages are needed. I think I will change my answer to four pages because I can put the three leftover cards on the fourth page even though it's not full." Student 4 says, "Can you show me another way to figure out how many pages are needed?" The student who started off the problem thinks about his new solution and proceeds to model it for the other students with a drawing.

Connection to Mathematics Standards

This FACT can be used to formatively assess students' understanding of any of the mathematics key ideas. It can be used with all the mathematical practices and especially provides an opportunity to use the mathematics practices of attending to precision when communicating mathematically, constructing viable arguments, and critiquing the reasoning of others.

General Implementation Attributes

Ease of Use: Easy   **Time Demand:** Medium
Cognitive Demand: Medium (depends on problem)

Modifications

The stems in the cards can be changed according to the type of problems in the problem set. It can be expanded to include fewer or more cards.

Caveats

This strategy should be modeled by the teacher first before students use it in small groups.

Use With Other Disciplines

This FACT can also be used in science, social studies, language arts, health, foreign languages, and visual and performing arts. For example, in science students can describe an experimental design for Cue Card 1, and the other students can use question stems on their cue cards to ask questions about the design of the experiment.

My Notes

_____

_____

_____

_____

_____

FACT 33

RANKING TASKS

Description

Ranking tasks are conceptual exercises first described by and used in physics education research (Maloney, 1987). Ranking tasks are based on a formative assessment technique called rule assessment (Siegler, 1976). The student is presented with a set of numbers, shapes, tables, graphs, diagrams, and so on that depict different variations of a situation or topic. For example, four different geometric solids with dimensions labeled, with some having similar dimensions, can be ranked according to their volume. The student then identifies the order of the ranking based on a certain outcome or result and describes the rule they used to determine the ranking. *Ranking Tasks* are often specifically designed to reveal research-identified misconceptions. Figure 3.27 shows an example of a *Ranking Task* used to uncover students' ideas about the rate of change. Students are asked to rank the six graphs from least to greatest rate of change, including rates of change that are equal.

A correct ranking of A = F < C = E < D < B and an explanation of how the student used rise/run, "up one over one," or the slope formula would reveal information about their conceptual understanding of rate of change. The task may reveal common misconceptions such as failure to understand how the scale of the x- and y-axis affect the rate of change represented in a graph.

How This FACT Promotes Student Learning

Ranking Tasks present a type of robust intellectual puzzle to students that cannot be solved by mere memorization of facts or mechanical use of formulas and equations. Students must think deeply and critically about the task to figure out what distinguishes one part from the others to come up with a sequence or ranking and a rule to explain the sequence or ranking. Through the use of different types of representations, ranking tasks encourage students to think about and analyze a concept in versatile ways. The use of visual representations helps them conceptualize abstract ideas. *Ranking Tasks* are often used as a set, beginning with a familiar concept or situation to engage students with what they already know and then build up, through careful scaffolding, to more complex ideas. Research studies have shown a positive effect on students' understanding when ranking tasks are used collaboratively (Hudgins et al., 2006).

Figure 3.27	Rate of Change

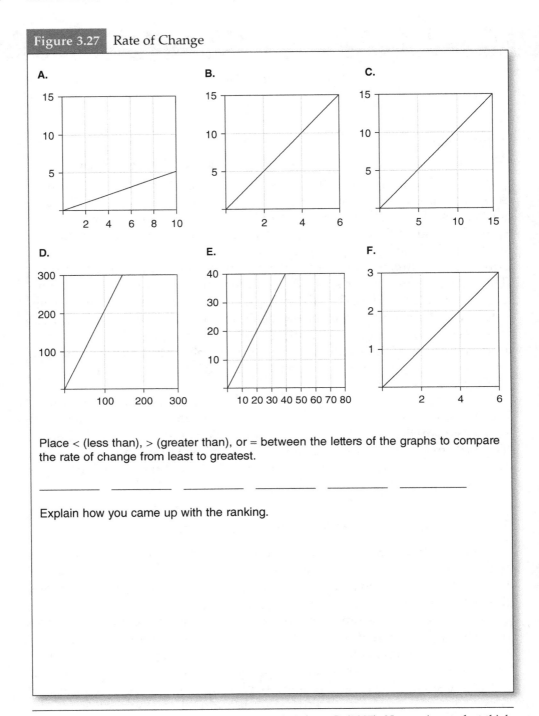

Place < (less than), > (greater than), or = between the letters of the graphs to compare the rate of change from least to greatest.

_____   _____   _____   _____   _____   _____

Explain how you came up with the ranking.

Source: Adapted from Rose, C. M., Minton, L., & Arline, C. (2007). _Uncovering student thinking in mathematics: 25 formative assessment probes_ (p. 106). Thousand Oaks, CA: Corwin.

How This FACT Informs Instruction

Ranking Tasks reveal information about students' understanding of a concept, use of mathematics language, awareness of variables that affect a situation, and ways in which they make conceptual linkages. Used as an elicitation, *Ranking Tasks* can reveal the extent of students' prior knowledge before designing instruction that draws on students' previous learning and experiences. *Ranking Tasks* are also used as checkpoints during instruction to see how students ideas are developing or changing. Ranking tasks can be used as pre- and post-formative assessments to check on the extent to which students' ideas have been changed by instruction and how students apply concepts they learned in new or novel ways. Since *Ranking Tasks* do not rely on memorized facts, formulas, and procedures and, instead, focus on conceptual understanding, they are especially useful in determining the extent to which instruction has succeeded in deepening understanding or changing students' initial ideas.

Design and Administration

Ranking Tasks are more suited to some concepts than others. Figures 3.27 and 3.28 show two ways a *Ranking Task* can be structured. If you plan to develop your own *Ranking Tasks*, suggestions for the basic structure of a *Ranking Task* includes the following four elements (Maloney, 1987):

1. A description of the context or problem, including any constraints, and how to rank the different figures, equations, or other representations.

2. A set of figures, equations, or other representations that show different arrangements of the situation to be compared and ranked.

3. A place to record the ranking for each figure, equations, or other representation.

4. A place to describe the rule or reasoning that was used to rank the figures, equations, or other representations.

Once students know how a *Ranking Task* works, the teacher can administer the tasks as individual or small-group paper-and-pencil assessments or use them to generate class discussions (O'Kuma, Maloney, & Hieggelke, 2000). A productive way to generate a class discussion is to give the class a *Ranking Task*, providing about 5 to 10 minutes to work on it and talk to each other in small groups about their rankings. Then ask selected individuals or groups to present their answers (small groups must come to a consensus on the best answer). If conflicting rankings have been presented to the class, have students defend their ideas. The teacher can then summarize the class ideas and guide students toward revising or refining their ideas and discovering the correct ranking.

Connection to Mathematics Standards

This FACT can be used to formatively assess students' understanding of any of the mathematics key ideas that lend themselves to ranking. It is especially useful in supporting the mathematical practice of reasoning abstractly and quantitatively.

General Implementation Attributes

Ease of Use: Medium   **Time Demand:** Medium   **Cognitive Demand:** High

Modifications

A modified version of *Ranking Tasks* can be developed and used without visual representations. For example, Figure 3.28 shows how a ranking task can be used with numeric representation. Sometimes, *Ranking Tasks* include a *Confidence Level Assessment* (FACT 3), where students are asked to rate how confident they are in their ranking.

Figure 3.28   Example of a Numeric Representation Ranking Task

Rank the numerical expressions. Use 1 for the smallest value and 5 for the great value.

$(-5)^2$ 5^{-2} -5^2 -5^{-2} $(-5)^{-2}$

_____   _____   _____   _____   _____

Explain why you ranked the expressions in this way.

Source: Adapted from Tobey, C. R., & Arline, C. (2009). *Uncovering student thinking in mathematics, grades 6–12: 30 formative assessment probes for the secondary classroom* (p. 71). Thousand Oaks, CA: Corwin.

Caveats

If students are new to *Ranking Tasks*, give them a sample practice task to work on first with a partner. Provide an opportunity to ask questions about how to answer the task. After they have worked on the task and discussed it with their partner, go over an example of what the best answer, including the explanation, would be and provide an opportunity to give and receive feedback on their sample tasks.

Use With Other Disciplines

This FACT can also be used in science. For example, students can be given a set of electrical circuit diagrams used to light identical lightbulbs and are asked to rank them according to the brightness of the bulbs in each circuit.

My Notes

_____

_____

_____

_____

_____

FACT 34

RAQ (REVISE, ADD, QUESTION) FEEDBACK

Description

Activating students as owners of their own learning and activating students as instructional resources for each other are two key aspects of formative assessment feedback (Wylie et al., 2012). The *RAQ (Revise, Add, Question) Feedback* FACT provides a scaffolded opportunity for students to support each other's learning through feedback on their mathematical models.

How This FACT Promotes Student Learning

Engaging students in providing feedback about each other's conceptual models promotes learning through carefully examining the ideas of others and comparing them to what is known about the mathematics being modeled. Furthermore, students who receive the peer feedback may be more apt to benefit from it, as feedback from peers is more likely to be given in language students understand (student-friendly feedback), which can then be more easily acted on and accepted. This FACT also supports student understanding of how to focus and give effective feedback through careful structuring, guidance, and modeling by the teacher. As a result, it improves students' ability to represent their mathematical models through drawings and other types of representations, as they learn from both suggesting changes to others' models and receiving suggestions to improve their own model. As students receive and consider feedback from each other, especially when accompanied by opportunities to present their models, it helps them reorganize their thinking and recognize when their ideas are changing, an important aspect of metacognition.

How This FACT Informs Instruction

RAQ Feedback is used when students are asked to represent their mathematical models through drawings or other types of visual representations. Students' initial mathematical models are meant to be changed. As students gain instructional experiences, they revisit their models to add new ideas or change aspects of their model. Teachers are not the only ones to provide feedback for students to improve their models. Students can participate in this role as well. As a result, the teacher gains valuable information on how students' mathematical models are changing by examining the feedback they are able to provide each other. Additionally, the teacher gains insight into student thinking from seeing the mathematical representation of their conceptual models and noting which suggestions from the feed-back students take into account and act on accordingly. If students' peer feedback fails to recognize critical aspects of the model that need to be modified or changed, this is an indication to the teacher that he or she will need to address this in subsequent instruction and class discussion of which mathematical models best represent the concept, idea, or problem.

Design and Administration

This FACT is used with mathematical models that make students' thinking visible and show how it changes over time. Students work in small groups, creating an initial representation (a type of model) in response to an elicitation about a concept or problem that is part of the big idea of an instructional unit. Students work together to create their initial model and explain it to the class. For example, students may be asked to create a graph that can be used to determine profit margins on several linear models to determine which product to sell. Students create representations of their linear models to illustrate why they choose a particular product.

After the models have been constructed, and students have had oppor-tunities to present and make additional revisions to their representations, the teacher plans instructional experiences that will address students' mis-understandings, flaws, or omissions in their models. Once students have gained knowledge that will prepare them to carefully reevaluate each other's models, they revisit the initial models using *RAQ Feedback*. Small groups are provided with three different colors of sticky notes to provide peer feedback on others' models. The teacher can decide how to assign which models students will evaluate, or small groups can exchange their model with another small group.

One color sticky note will be used for "R" feedback. R feedback is given when a part of a model needs to be revised (partially or completely changed). For example, one group might provide the following feedback: "Your intervals are not consistent for the dependent variable. You should change it so that the intervals are equivalent." "A" feedback is given when something is missing and needs to be added to a model. For example, one group might post, "Your profit margin line for T-shirts is labeled, but the other two are not. Labeling each of the other lines would help show the difference between T-shirts, sweatshirts, and posters more clearly." "Q" feedback is given when students wish to pose a question for consideration. For example, a group might post, "Have you thought about changing the scale to better highlight the different profit margins?" Color coding and defining the type of feedback scaffold the process of providing useful peer feedback. The students write their feedback suggestion on the respective sticky note and attach it to the representation so the group that developed the model can consider the feedback and revise or refine their model, with-out the feedback being directly written on the drawing.

Before students revisit and improve their representations, the teacher may wish to review the feedback first for (1) the opportunity to gain insight into the class's thinking based on the feedback they provide; (2) examining the extent to which students are able to provide useful feedback; (3) removing or addressing feedback that would not improve a group's model, especially feedback that would support or add a misconception; and (4) additional feedback the teacher could add to help students improve their models, using the same coding. The teacher may choose to review the feedback with students during class.

Once the teacher determines that the feedback is useful and has added teacher feedback as needed, students consider the feedback (if useful) to make changes to their model, incorporating what they learned during the activities and discussions designed to address students' initial ideas. Once students have made changes, the teacher, with the class, can generate a whole-class consensus model that incorporates the feedback given to small-group models.

Connection to Mathematics Standards

This FACT can be used to provide students with feedback on their understanding of any mathematics key ideas. It is particularly useful in providing feedback on the mathematical practice of modeling.

General Implementation Attributes

Ease of Use: Medium   **Time Demand:** High   **Cognitive Demand:** High

Modifications

Depending on the stage of instruction and the extent of knowledge students must have to provide correct and useful feedback, the teacher can use the same RAQ codes to provide teacher to student feedback. The R can be modified to provide positive feedback in which the R represents "Right on!"

Caveats

Make sure the feedback provided does not encourage students to change a correct or partially correct model to an incorrect model based on a misconception. You might consider "traffic lighting" the feedback for students after they post it, with colored marks or stick on dots added by the teacher: red—do not use this feedback and discuss with your group why you should not use this feedback, yellow—carefully consider this feedback and discuss it with your group first, and green—use this feedback and discuss with your group why this is good feedback.

Use With Other Disciplines

This FACT can also be used in science to provide feedback on students' conceptual models of phenomena. For example, students may be asked to draw a representation of what is happening to the particles in a glass of water as matter changes state from a liquid to a gas.

My Notes

_____

_____

_____

_____

_____

FACT 35

REFLECT ALOUD

Description

Reflect Aloud (Creighton et al., 2015) is a way for teachers to model for students how to reflect on their learning in relation to the *Learning Intention* and *Success Indicators*. In this FACT, the teacher represents a sample student in the class when he or she reflects aloud about understanding the *Learning Intention* and *Success Indicators*, modeling for students the kind of internal dialogue that goes on in a self-assessment reflection.

How This FACT Promotes Student Learning

Reflect Aloud helps develop students' ability to articulate their own self-assessments of their learning by hearing and seeing the modeling of a sample internal dialogue. This strategy focuses students' attention on the use of *Success Indicators* as a basis for evaluating their own learning.

How This FACT Informs Instruction

The *Reflect Aloud* can sometimes serve the dual purpose of also reviewing some of the key ideas of the lesson. It can also transition into an opportunity for the teacher to give whole-class feedback on the success criteria.

Design and Administration

Figure 3.29 shows the steps for this FACT. An example is provided at each step, using the sample *Learning Intention* and *Success Indicators* for a lesson.

Learning Intention: By the end of the lesson, you will understand <u>why</u> the area of any triangle is $\frac{1}{2}bh$.

> *Success Indicator 1:* I can relate the shape of a triangle to the shape of a rectangle with the same base and height.

> *Success Indicator 2:* I can explain why the area of a triangle is half the area of a rectangle with the same base and height for right triangles, acute triangles, and obtuse triangles.

| Figure 3.29 | Steps of *Reflect Aloud* |

Step in Reflect Aloud	What the Teacher Might Say
Step 1: Review one of the *Success Indicators*, and reflect aloud how to rephrase the success indicator into your own words.	Let's see . . . the first success indicator says that I can relate the shape of a triangle to the shape of a rectangle with the same base and height. So that means when I've got these two shapes and they have the same base and height, I need to be able to compare the way the triangle looks—or relates to—the way the rectangle looks.
Step 2: Describe a self-assessment of "your" ability to meet the success indicator, representing what you consider to be the majority of the class. Your description of what "you" can do (that is, what you expect most of your students can do) also serves as a summary of some key ideas of the lesson.	I'm pretty sure I can do that. I can see that sometimes the shape of the triangle fits in half of the rectangle. For other triangles (points to diagrams on the board of acute triangles), I can see that if I cut up the triangle and rearrange the pieces, I can make a triangle that's still half a rectangle. But I'm really not very sure yet what to do with these kinds of triangles (points to obtuse triangles drawn on the board for which the height is outside the interior of the triangle) because I'm not sure how to cut them to rearrange the pieces in the same way, and I'm not sure what the height is.
Step 3: Check your "dialogue" with your students to see who feels the dialogue represents them reasonably accurately.	Who feels like that's what they could say about themselves for that success indicator? (A number of hands go up.) For others who didn't feel like that dialogue fit them, what would be different for you? (Students offer comments, and teacher rephrases as needed to model language of self-assessment.)
Step 4: Repeats Steps 1–3 with the remaining *Success Indicators*.	
Step 5: Summarize a self-assessment of the *Learning Intention*.	I feel like I'm meeting the first and second success indicators for many triangles, but there are certain triangles for which I'm still unsure what to do. In terms of the learning intention, I think I'm understanding why the area is $\frac{1}{2}$ base times height <u>some</u> of the time. But for some other examples, I'm still figuring out why this works.

Connection to Mathematics Standards

This FACT can be used to provide students with feedback on their understanding of any of the mathematics key ideas as well as their use of any of the mathematics practices.

General Implementation Attributes

Ease of Use: Medium   **Time Demand:** Medium
Cognitive Demand: High

Modifications

Reflect Aloud can be paired effectively with the *Take Stock* FACT (see FACT 44). This FACT can be particularly effective at a midway point in a lesson as well as at the end of a lesson. As students become familiar with the FACT, consider calling on a student to do the *reflect aloud*. You could model one *Success Indicator* and ask students to *reflect aloud* as partners for the second success indicator. Think about ways to gradually release responsibility for the reflection to students so that they can *reflect aloud* in pairs without the teacher modeling the strategy.

Caveats

As with other strategies, there is a risk of overusing this FACT so that listening to it becomes tedious for students.

Use With Other Disciplines

This FACT can also be used in science, social studies, language arts, health, foreign languages, and visual and performing arts. For example, a science teacher might use this FACT to do model reflection on a *Learning Intention* and *Success Indicators* that address designing a carefully controlled experiment.

My Notes

FACT 36

REFLECT THEN SELF-ASSESS

Description

Many self-assessment strategies require students to rate their understanding and then provide evidence of their learning. *Reflect Then Self-Assess* purposefully switches the order using a process that first has students reflect on what they were doing before having students rate the extent of their understanding during a problem-solving practice set.

How This FACT Promotes Student Learning

Reflect Then Self-Assess promotes metacognition and helps students gauge their current learning status during a problem-solving practice set. Too often, students assess progress on the completion of tasks rather than on the quality of the response to the task or whether they did the intellectual work themselves. This FACT prompts students to think about quality and ownership prior to assigning a rating to their progress. They must first reflect on what they could do successfully or needed help on as well as how they helped others before considering the extent to which they think they successfully completed a task.

How This FACT Informs Instruction

This FACT enables teachers to hear or read the students' own accounts of how they think their learning is progressing. Reviewing the types of mistakes students describe, what they can do successfully, what they needed help with, or how they can help others provides useful information the teacher can use to determine next instructional steps, including how to pair students for further support.

Design and Administration

Determine a set of reflection prompts and rating questions appropriate for the task students will complete. After students have completed the task, ask students to reflect then assess. For example, Figure 3.30 shows an example problem-solving template after fourth-grade students have completed a set of items on adding decimals during independent, paired, or group work. This template is available at www.uncoveringstudentideas.org/templates.

Connection to Mathematics Standards

This FACT can be used to formatively assess students' understanding of any of the mathematics key ideas. It is especially useful in formatively

Figure 3.30 *Reflect Then Self-Assess* for a Math Problem Set

What I practiced:

My reflection:

How I think I did:

☐ I solved all the problems correctly without needing any help. I can help others with these kinds of problems.

☐ I solved all the problems correctly. I can work through these kinds of problems without help.

☐ I solved the problems correctly after getting some help. I think I can work through these kinds of problems on my own now.

☐ I solved most of these problems after getting some help. I think I still need help with these kinds of problems.

Comments:

A copy of this template can be downloaded at www.uncoveringstudentideas.org/templates.

assessing the mathematical practice of making sense of problems and persevering in solving them.

General Implementation Attributes

Ease of Use: Medium   **Time Demand:** Medium
Cognitive Demand: Medium

Modifications

To help scaffold the reflection part of this FACT, provide students with a scaffold such as the following:

- What I did well
- What I struggled with
- Mistakes I made
- What help I needed
- What kind of help I got
- What help I was able to give others

Caveats

Consider using a *Reflect Aloud* (see FACT 35) to model *Reflect Then Self-Assess* for students.

Use With Other Disciplines

This FACT can also be used in science, social studies, language arts, health, foreign languages, and visual and performing arts. For example, in language arts students can use this strategy to reflect and then assess how they did on a set of punctuation exercises where they had to determine where to place commas.

My Notes

_____

_____

_____

_____

_____

FACT 37

"RULES THAT EXPIRE" PROBES

Description

In the *13 Rules That Expire* article (Karp, Bush, & Dougherty, 2014), the authors point out rules that seem to hold true at the moment, given the content the student is learning. However, students later find that these rules are not always true; in fact, these rules expire. Such experiences can be frustrating and, in students' minds, can further the notion that mathematics is a mysterious series of tricks and tips to memorize rather than big concepts that relate to one another (Karp et al., 2014). The *"Rules That Expire" Probes* uncover whether students use an incorrect rule or overgeneralization to apply a mathematical idea.

How This FACT Promotes Student Learning

"Rules That Expire" Probes activate student thinking about a particular algorithm, rule, procedure, definition, or concept they learned about in prior instruction. The probe encourages them to think about different contexts in which they can apply their mathematical ideas.

How This FACT Informs Instruction

"Rules That Expire" Probes help teachers identify areas where students make incorrect generalizations that often remain hidden unless the teacher uses specific strategies to surface them. Once these overgeneralizations are identified, teachers can select appropriate strategies to help students understand when a rule, definition, algorithm, symbol, or other mathematical idea or representation applies or does not apply in a given context.

Design and Administration

In *"Rules That Expire" Probes*, students are given two or more examples that have some similarity to the targeted mathematical concept or idea and are asked to select the examples that match a given situation, word, or concept. The distracters selected should have the potential to reveal a lack of conceptual understanding or misinterpretation of a rule. Students are asked to provide a justification for the examples they selected. For example, the probe item shown in Figure 3.31 addresses the rule "two negatives make a positive." This is true when two negative numbers are multiplied or divided but may be misapplied in other operations.

| Figure 3.31 | Example *"Rules That Expire" Probe* |

Is It Positive?

Without actually calculating, use reasoning to determine whether the expression results in a POSITIVE answer.

Circle Yes or No.	Explain your choice.
a. $-(-53.4 + 92.3)$ Yes　　　No	
b. $-34.23 - 27.9$ Yes　　　No	

Source: Tobey, C. R., & Arline, C. (2014a). *Uncovering student thinking about mathematics in the Common Core, grades 6–8: 25 formative assessment probes* (p. 49). Thousand Oaks, CA: Corwin. Used with permission.

Connection to Mathematics Standards

This FACT can be used to formatively assess students' understanding of any of the mathematics key ideas. It is especially useful in supporting the mathematical practices of reasoning abstractly and quantitatively, looking for and making use of structure, and looking for and expressing regularity in repeated reasoning.

General Implementation Attributes

Ease of Use: Medium　　　**Time Demand:** Medium
Cognitive Demand: Medium/High

Modifications

Consider leaving a blank box for students to write in their own example.

Caveats

Be sure to provide a follow-up experience so that students recognize the incorrect application of the targeted mathematical idea and can work through their misunderstandings.

Use With Other Disciplines

This FACT can also be used in science. For example, in science if students are given a list of shiny and non-shiny objects and asked to select which objects can reflect light, they may choose only the shiny objects. This may stem from the use of mirrors during reflection activities that may result in students applying an incorrect generalization regarding the properties of objects that can reflect light.

My Notes

_____

_____

_____

_____

_____

FACT 38

SEEING STRUCTURE

Description

Seeing Structure is a FACT that requires students to solve a set of problems by seeing a common structure within the items in the set. When students see and use structure they notice patterns in symbolic or graphical representations and understand these patterns as both single objects as well as compositions of objects. Most important, they can use their understanding of these compositions of objects to solve a problem or series of related problems.

How This FACT Promotes Student Learning

Looking for structure can help students learn to solve problems more efficiently. By asking students to look for structure in solving problems, and communicating those ideas with others, students will better understand how seeing structure can vary both within a problem and across problems. For example, students have a better chance of success at finding equivalent expressions to 3×18 if they understand the structure of multiplication in terms of the distributive property. Students can more readily see expressions such as $3 \times 10 + 3 \times 8$ as equivalent to 3×18 if they have had experiences that allow them to internalize the structure of the distributive property through use of an area model.

How This FACT Informs Instruction

By providing opportunities and using a series of problems that rely on the same structure, teachers are better able to formatively assess students' ability to look for and make use of structure. The *Seeing Structure* FACT such as the example in Figure 3.32, allows the teacher to formatively assess this skill by looking for students' selections and explanations that show understanding of the structure of the distributive property rather than having to procedurally calculate the value of each expression.

Design and Administration

Develop a question with several correct answer choices that can be determined using structure rather than procedure. Include several nonexamples students may be likely to choose that would uncover common difficulties or misconceptions (see Figure 3.32).

Figure 3.32	Equivalent Expressions

Circle each expression that is equivalent to 4 × 13.

4 × 10 + 3   2 × 10 + 2 × 3   4 × 8 + 5

2 × 8 + 2 × 5   4 × 10 + 1 × 3   2 × 10 + 2 × 3

Explain your thinking:

Another way to design *Seeing Structure* probes is to develop two to four selected response items that each rely on a common structure such as in Figure 3.33. The *Scatterplots* probe shown in Figure 3.33 was designed to formatively assess whether students are able to see the structure of a group of data as having positive, negative or no correlation regardless of how the data cluster appears in the coordinate plane (i.e., in one quadrant or across two or more quadrants). Provide a space for students to explain their thinking. The explanation is key to determining whether, in fact, students are seeing structure and are able to explain or articulate the reasons for their selected answer choices by using that structure.

Connection to Mathematics Standards

This FACT can be used to formatively assess students' understanding of any of the mathematics key ideas. It is especially useful in providing an opportunity for students to use the mathematics practices of making sense of problems and persevering in solving them and looking for and making use of structure.

Figure 3.33 *Scatterplots* Probe for *Seeing Structure*

Scatterplots

Determine whether the data in each scatterplot shows a positive, negative, or no correlation or whether there isn't enough information to determine the correlation.

Circle the correct answer.	Explain your choice.
1. 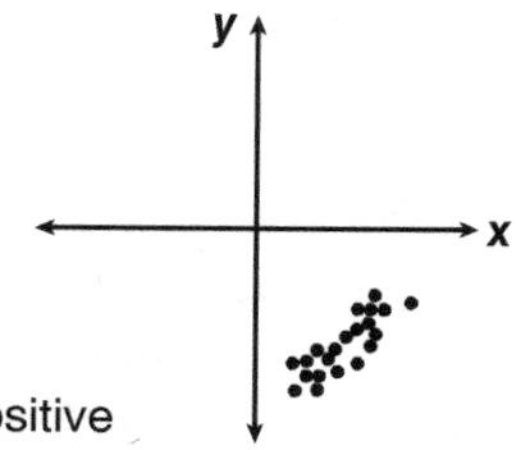 a. Positive b. Negative c. No correlation d. Not enough information	
2. 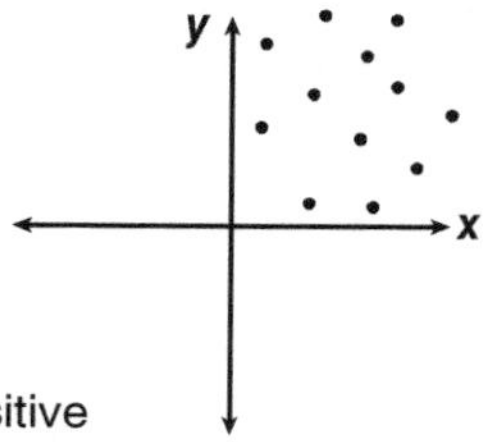 a. Positive b. Negative c. No correlation d. Not enough information	
3. 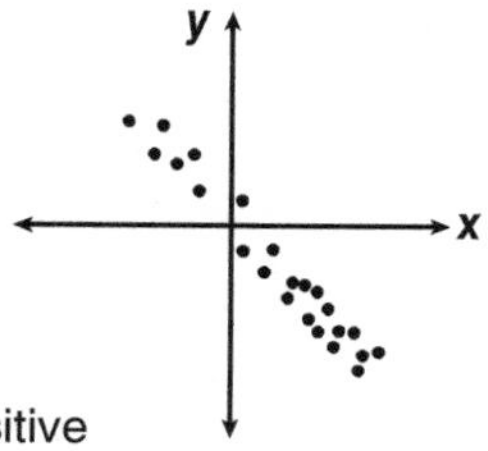 a. Positive b. Negative c. No correlation d. Not enough information	

Source: Tobey, C. R., & Arline, C. (2014a). *Uncovering student thinking about mathematics in the Common Core, grades 6–8: 25 formative assessment probes* (p. 131). Thousand Oaks, CA: Corwin. Used with permission.

General Implementation Attributes

Ease of Use: Medium   **Time Demand:** Medium   **Cognitive Demand:** High

Modifications

Seeing Structure probes can also be created as a categorical card sort in which students sort examples that have a common structure into categories, using structure to explain the categories.

Caveats

Be sure to vary the types of problems when requiring students to use structure. Don't limit this FACT to just one area of mathematics. *Seeing Structure* probes should be developed and used across the content domains of mathematics.

Use With Other Disciplines

This FACT is specific to mathematics.

My Notes

_____

_____

_____

_____

_____

FACT 39

SLIDE SORT

Description

Slide Sorts are similar to *Card Sorts* (Keeley & Tobey, 2011) in that students sort examples by designated categories. Unlike a card sort where the students manipulate a set of cards, the *Slide Sort* strategy presents one example at a time as a slide show, using PowerPoint, Keynote, or other presentation software, with the teacher controlling the order in which the students view the examples on the slides.

How This FACT Promotes Student Learning

Slide Sorts provide an opportunity for students to activate their thinking as they access their prior knowledge, review material they learned, or apply their learning to new examples. The pictorial nature of this probe supports visual learners as well as ELLs. Seeing a larger image often triggers ideas that may not surface from text or small pictures on cards. As students progress through the slides, their thinking may change as they view a variety of examples. As students work in pairs or small groups to share how they sorted the examples on the slides, they put forth their own ideas for others to consider, strengthen their skills of explaining and justifying their thinking, evaluate the ideas of others, and modify their own thinking as new information convinces them to reconsider their original sort. *Slide Sorts* can also be used to help students revisit material they learned previously to scaffold their learning for the next lesson.

How This FACT Informs Instruction

Slide Sorts provide a way for the teacher to elicit students' preconceptions, assess students' ability to transfer knowledge when provided with new examples or contexts, and look for areas of uncertainty or disagreement among students that may signify the need for further instructional opportunities. Because the order is controlled by the teacher, progressively more challenging examples or examples that are very different can be revealed at different places within the sequence of slides. While students discuss their ideas, the teacher is listening to students as they agree, disagree, or express their uncertainty. By observing cross-outs on the students' recording sheets, the teacher can observe how students' ideas are changing through discussion. The teacher notes examples that students may not agree on or sort incorrectly to address in subsequent lessons or during class discussion.

Design and Administration

Choose a topic or concept that can be represented with visual images. Select 12 to 20 images, depending on the concept. Using PowerPoint, Keynote, or other presentation software, create a set of slides with the labeled images. Arrange the slides in an order that begins with familiar examples to students and progresses to include more challenging examples or ones that are likely to bring to the surface common misconceptions. Intersperse examples students are likely to know throughout the sequence. For example, a *Slide Sort* is used to elicit students' thinking about parallelograms and whether the information provided about the sides and angles is enough to determine whether a two-dimensional shape is a parallelogram. One at a time, a two-dimensional shape (see examples in Figure 3.34) is projected on the screen. Students individually determine whether the information provided can be used to determine whether the shape is a parallelogram.

Begin this FACT by having each student individually record the examples and nonexamples for the concept selected. Using the template in Figure 3.35, students list which slides are examples of a parallelogram and which slides are not examples of a parallelogram. They then describe the rule, definition, or reasoning used to decide which slides belong in which category (a copy of this template can be downloaded at www.uncovering

Figure 3.34   Examples of Visuals Used for a *Slide Sort*

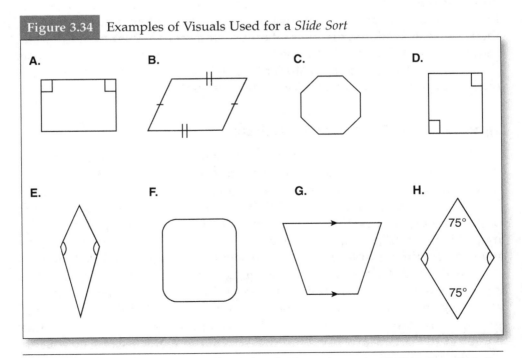

Source: Rose, C. M., Minton, L., & Arline, C. (2007). *Uncovering student thinking in mathematics: 25 formative assessment probes* (p. 163). Thousand Oaks, CA: Corwin. Used with permission.

Figure 3.35 Recording Sheet for *Slide Sort*

Slide Sort for _____	
Examples	**Nonexamples**
The rule I used to sort the slides:	

A copy of this template can be downloaded at www.uncoveringstudentideas.org/templates.

studentideas.org/templates). Show the slides one at a time, with approximately 5 to 10 seconds between each one.

After all the slides have been shown and individual students have recorded their answers, have them form pairs or small groups to compare and discuss their *Slide Sort*. Students can now change their answers. Encourage students to put a line through the answer they change and add to the other category so there is a record of which things they thought differently about after they saw all the slides and discussed their ideas. Then have students write the rule, the reasoning, or the definition they used for their sort.

Listen for examples that challenged students' thinking or ones about which they did not agree. For example, when students see the slide with Example A, they may assume it is a parallelogram since visually it does look like one. But the correct answer is there is not enough information. One does not know for sure if the other two angles are right angles. They could be 89.5 degrees and 90.5 degrees, too small a difference to detect visually. Use the information to plan further instruction that will refine or solidify students' thinking. Revisit the slides with the class either at the end of the lesson or in a series of lessons to determine the extent to which the class now understands the concept and can apply a mathematical definition, a rule, or a reasoning.

Connection to Mathematics Standards

This FACT can be used with any of the key mathematics ideas that can be represented with visual images. It supports the practice of constructing viable arguments and critiquing the reasoning of others because students discuss each slide and defend their reasons for the placement. It also supports the practice of attending to precision because students use precise language in communicating their ideas.

General Implementation Attributes

Ease of Use: High   **Time Demand:** Medium   **Cognitive Demand:** Medium

Modifications

Justified List Probes can be turned into *Slide Sorts* (Keeley & Tobey, 2011). This strategy can be used with the *Group Frayer Model* (see FACT 18); the examples on the slides are used for the bottom half of the Frayer chart. Use fewer slides with younger children.

Caveats

Make sure the pictures and examples used for the slides are familiar to students. Provide enough time between slides for students to think and record their answers but not too much time that they get restless.

Use With Other Disciplines

This FACT can also be used in science, social studies, language arts, foreign languages, health, and performing arts. For example, in social studies students might sort objects into things that were first invented by the ancient Chinese to understand that many technologies modern society uses are based on technological achievements of ancient China.

My Notes

_____

_____

_____

_____

_____

FACT 40

SORT ENVELOPES

Description

Sort Envelopes is an organization method for collecting the results of a Card Sort (Keeley & Tobey, 2011) in which elementary students sort a set of cards with pictures, numbers, symbols, or words according to a specific characteristic or category. Students sort the cards based on their prior knowledge about the concept or procedure. The envelopes serve as category cards, and after sorting all the cards, students place the cards into the envelopes for safekeeping.

How This FACT Promotes Student Learning

Sort Envelopes provides an opportunity for elementary students to access their prior knowledge and reflect on their learning. In addition, the sorting process promotes metacognition by surfacing what they think they understand as well as any uncertainties in their thinking. Returning to the sorted cards after instruction allows students to make changes based on new understanding gained during instruction.

How This FACT Informs Instruction

Card Sorts provide a way for the teacher to elicit elementary students' preconceptions, assess students' ability to transfer knowledge when provided with new examples or contexts, and look for areas of uncertainty or disagreement among students that may signify the need for further instructional opportunities. By observing as students lay out their cards, the teacher gains specific insights into students' levels of understanding. By using *Sort Envelopes*, the teacher can later review a subset of students' sorts to plan next steps.

Design and Administration

The first time this FACT is used, prepare enough envelopes so each student has a small manila envelope and at least two small letter envelopes (see Figure 3.36). Prepare sets of cards that align with the content goal of the lesson or cluster of lessons students will encounter. A *Justified List* probe (Keeley & Tobey, 2011) can be easily turned into a *Card Sort* by placing each of the statements, words, numbers, symbols, or shapes listed on a card. (See the Appendix for a source of assessment probes that can be used as card sorts.) Figure 3.37 is an example of a card set used by first graders with the *Sort Envelopes* FACT. You can place text on index cards or

Figure 3.36 | Example of a *Sort Envelope*

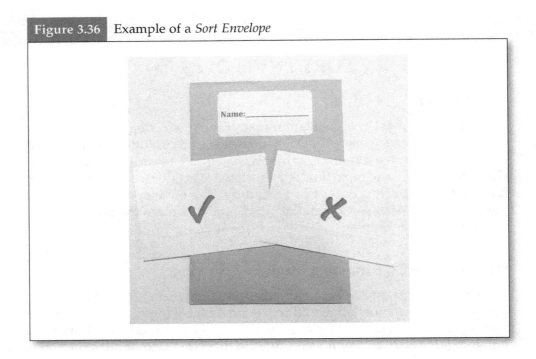

make cards from preprinted matchbook-sized squares on a sheet of paper, cut out and sorted into ziplock bags (or have students cut out the squares). Provide students with category headers for their envelopes. Encourage students to lay out the cards in a row or column under the category header rather than on top of each other so you can see how students sort each individual card.

After the sort, have students place their cards in the small envelope that matches each category. Put the small envelopes in the manila envelope, collect the envelopes, and proceed with your next instructional steps. When you feel the students are ready to revisit their ideas, reflect, and resort, return the envelopes to the students. The following vignette highlights the use of *Sort Envelopes* by a third-grade teacher:

> Sorts are one of my favorite types of formative assessment techniques. I find they are engaging for all students and particularly helpful for students who struggle to write their ideas on paper and pencil. I recently had my students complete an addition card sort as an individual activity before we began a unit of study on fractions. I made observations during the sort. I sometimes asked students to explain to me how they sorted. I also asked students to use a blank card to write one pair of equivalent fractions.

I use an envelope system that allows me to keep track of each student's sorted cards. At the beginning of the school year, I give each student a small reclosable 6 × 9 manila envelope along with small letter envelopes labeled "yes" and "no." Students write their names on the manila envelopes and decorate them. When we do a card sort, they place their cards in the small envelopes and put those in the manila envelope.

This system works great for me. If I am not able to make it around to all my students during the sort, I can review their cards later. Having the sets of sorted cards enables me to follow up with students, share information with special education teachers, plan learning targets and create pairings for subsequent lessons. (Tobey & Fagan, 2014, pp. 193–194)

| Figure 3.37 | Example of Cards Used With *Sort Envelopes* |

Sums of Ten

8 + 2	3 + 7		5 + 5	2 + 6 + 3
6 + 4	4 + ⠿		5 + 1 + 4	⠢ + 8
1 + ⠿⠿	2 + 7 + 1		⠿ + ⠿	9 + 1
⠿ + ⠢	7 + 5		10 + 0	3 + 4 + 4

Source: Tobey, C. R., & Fagan, E. (2013). *Uncovering student thinking about mathematics in the Common Core, grades K–2: 20 formative assessment probes* (p. 109). Thousand Oaks, CA: Corwin. Used with permission.

Connection to Mathematics Standards

This FACT can be used to formatively assess students' understanding of any of the key ideas in mathematics. It also provides an opportunity to use any of the mathematical practices.

General Implementation Attributes

Ease of Use: Medium   **Time Demand:** Medium
Cognitive Demand: Medium

Modifications

Sort Envelopes can be exchanged with other students for providing feedback on each other's sort.

Caveats

This FACT is best used with elementary students.

Use With Other Disciplines

This FACT can also be used in science, social studies, language arts, health, foreign languages, and visual and performing arts for any type of card sort assessment. For example, in language arts students can use a *Sort Envelope* to sort words into two- and three-syllable words.

My Notes

_____

_____

_____

_____

_____

FACT 41

STRUCTURES FOR TAKING ACTION

Description

Structures for Taking Action is a self-assessment and feedback FACT. It provides hints students can use for self-regulation and internal feedback. It is important for students to take part in their own learning; to know when they aren't fully understanding the mathematics and know what kind of action they can take to help them understand. This FACT helps students self-monitor and then choose an action that will help them learn when they feel stuck. It also helps them think about what to do with the feedback they get externally.

How This FACT Promotes Student Learning

One of the goals of formative assessment is to activate students as owners of their own learning, thus supporting metacognition. Too often, self-assessment is a tokenistic add-on to the end of the lesson, where teachers ask students to show a color; number of fingers; thumbs up, down, or sideways; or other signals to show the extent to which they understand the content of the lesson, and nothing happens as a result (Wiliam & Leahy, 2015). The same is often true of feedback. Students are given feedback but there is no or little follow-up in how to use the feedback. With this FACT, students who are stuck can choose an action they can take to move their learning forward or use the feedback they get externally more productively. It also supports a skill students can use for life when they struggle with a real-life problem.

A problem with feedback is that sometimes students do not know what to do with the feedback they receive. Struggling students are reluctant to take action without the teacher's guidance and step-by-step support and other students lack confidence to take next steps. Helping students focus on a hint or cue encourages self-direction and provides the initial guidance they need to choose an action.

How This FACT Informs Instruction

Teachers do their best to meet the needs of all students as much as possible. However, a truly effective teacher helps students learn how to be monitors and activators of their own learning. When students learn how to help themselves by first using the resources that are available to them, they are much more precise when asking for external help, thus freeing the teacher to help students who need it the most.

Design and Administration

To help students move their learning forward when they are stuck or have received external feedback but are not sure what to do about it, create two lists of things students can do and make the list available to them. One list includes the things students can do by themselves when they feel stuck. Include on the list specific resources students might have available in the classroom. The second list includes the things students can do with the feedback they receive. Figure 3.38 shows an example of a bulletin board chart in a classroom for students to refer to when they are stuck or have received feedback on their work and wonder what to do next (Creighton et al., 2015). As students work on a problem check to see how

---

Figure 3.38   *Structures for Taking Action* Bulletin Board

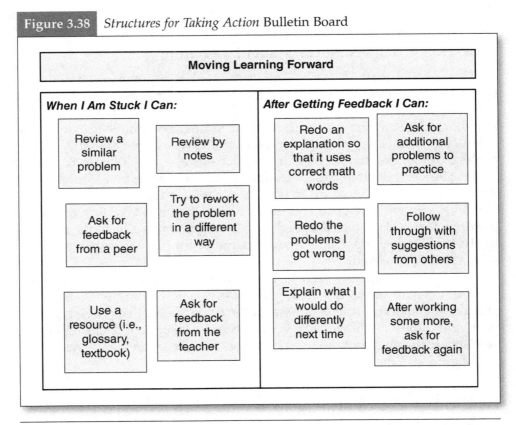

Source: Creighton, S. J., Tobey, C. R., Karnowski, E., & Fagan, E. (2015). *Bringing math students into the formative assessment equation: Tools and strategies for the middle grades* (p. 182). Thousand Oaks, CA: Corwin. Used with permission.

they are using the suggestions on the chart and add additional ones that may needed.

Connection to Mathematics Standards

This FACT can be used to help students use feedback related to any of the key ideas in mathematics. It also provides an opportunity to support any of the mathematical practices.

General Implementation Attributes

Ease of Use: Medium   **Time Demand:** Medium
Cognitive Demand: Medium

Modifications

Customize the list according to the resources available to students in the classroom. Teachers can also use the list to suggest actions initially until students are familiar with using the suggestions. For example, in a fourth-grade classroom students are comparing metric units of measurement. The teacher notices that several students are having problems comparing 2 kilograms to 500 grams and seem to focus more on the magnitude of the numbers. She points to the chart and says, "I see that some of you are having problems with 3. I think you might have something in your math notebook that can help you. Look through the notes you made yesterday to see if you can find a similar problem we did that could help you with this one." Over time, the teacher can gradually turn the decision over to the students to decide on an action to take.

Caveats

This FACT is only useful if time is provided for students to use the suggestions to work on problems they are struggling with or to use feedback to revise or improve their work.

Use With Other Disciplines

This FACT can also be used in science, social studies, language arts, health, foreign language, and performing arts. For example, a language arts teacher may use this FACT to design a bulletin board that will help students with their writing tasks.

My Notes

FACT 42

SUCCESS INDICATORS

Description

Success Indicators are used with *Learning Intentions* (FACT 23) as a strategy to help students and teachers gauge the extent to which a learning goal has been met. They are sometimes referred to as "I can" statements or success criteria. *Success Indicators* are shared (and sometimes developed) with students so they can take responsibility for monitoring their own learning.

How This FACT Promotes Student Learning

Since state standards are often written in formal language, primarily for teachers, writing *Learning Intentions* and *Success Indicators* in student-friendly language helps clarify what they are expected to learn. *Success Indicators* help students understand what it means to meet the *Learning Intention* by breaking it down into tangible and measureable sub-goals so students can take responsibility for their own learning during a lesson or task. Students can self-monitor whether they are successfully learning and whether they may need help from other students or the teacher. Benefits to using *Success Indicators* with students are the following:

- Having the appropriate focus while engaged in an activity or task
- Using the indicators as the focus for self-assessment and self-monitoring during an activity or a task and after completion
- Providing indicators for peer assessment and peer feedback so that students know what to focus on when sharing their work
- Helping students develop a sense of what is and what is not important during the learning process (Clarke, 2005)

How This FACT Informs Instruction

The process of determining the *Success Indicators* for a *Learning Intention* helps teachers focus on what students need to know and do during a lesson to show evidence that they have met the *Learning Intention*. It helps define the parts of a lesson that contribute to learning and ensure that the lesson or task will provide an opportunity to learn, as well as provide evidence of learning. It helps teachers move from an activity focus to a learning focus. Once *Success Indicators* are developed, teachers can then identify which FACTs can be used to elicit the evidence that students have successfully met the criteria for the *Success Indicators*. As teachers check on the extent to which students met the *Success Indicators*, it feeds back into the lesson so teachers can adjust the lesson or task accordingly or plan for additional learning opportunities that students might need before moving on to the next *Learning Intention*.

Design and Administration

Success Indicators are used with *Learning Intentions* (FACT 23). At the beginning of the lesson, the *Learning Intention* and *Success Indicators* should be posted and communicated to students. It is important to make sure students understand the *Success Indicators* prior to undertaking the activity or task. The indicators should be written in language appropriate for the students' grade level. Students can help generate the *Success Indicators*. Students should be encouraged to refer to the *Success Indicators* as they engage in the learning process. *Success Indicators* can be scaffolded, so parts of the lesson link increasingly complex ideas, which, when clustered, make up the *Learning Intention*.

Sometimes formative assessment probes and FACTs reveal gaps in students' understanding or misconceptions that need to be addressed during the learning process. The information from these formative assessments can feed into the development of *Learning Intentions* and *Success Indicators* to monitor the extent to which the gap has been filled or the misconception has been given up in favor of the scientific idea.

Success Indicators are also used at the end of the lesson to have students self-assess the extent to which they think they met the indicator, using quick FACTs such as *Thumbs Up, Thumbs Down* (Keeley & Tobey, 2011). This helps the teacher ascertain whether the class or certain students are ready to move on to the next *Learning Intention* or scaffolded *Success Indicator* and which students need a responsive action. The *Success Indicators* can also be used to have students peer assess and provide feedback on the student work that results from the lesson.

Success Indicators in mathematics should include one or more indicators related to the mathematics processes practices. Sentence starters for developing *Success Indicators* include

- I can identify . . .
- I can use a model to . . .
- I can explain why . . .
- I can carry out a math investigation to . . .
- I can distinguish between ___ and ___
- I can develop a . . .
- I can solve . . .
- I can generate questions about . . .

- I can design a . . .
- I can define . . .
- I can graph . . .
- I can find . . .
- I can calculate . . .
- I can construct an argument about . . .
- I can provide evidence for . . .
- I can use _____ to . . .
- I can prove that . . .
- I can compare . . .

The following are examples of *Success Indicators* developed for various lessons across grade spans:

Grade K–2:

Learning Intention: I understand partial sums as a strategy for adding two numbers.

> *Success Indicator 1:* I can solve addition problems using the partial sum strategy.

> *Success Indicator 2:* I can describe or show why the partial sum strategy works.

Grade 3–5

Learning Intention: I understand use of the distributive property as a strategy for multiplication.

> *Success Indicator 1:* I can apply the distributive property to multiply two or more factors.

> *Success Indicator 2:* I can use an area model to explain or show why the distributive property works.

Grade 6–8

Learning Intention: What does it mean for two sets of numbers in a table to be proportional to each other?

> *Success Indicator 1:* I can find a pair of numbers that are proportional to a given pair.

> *Success Indicator 2:* I can use words, graphs, or other pictures to show whether two sets of numbers in a table are proportional to each other.

Grade 9–12

Learning Intention: Whether a product is rational or irrational can be determined by the factors involved.

Success Indicator 1: I can determine whether a product is rational or irrational based on the factors.

Success Indicator 2: I can explain or show why the product of two irrational numbers can be either rational or irrational.

Success Indicator 3: I can explain or show when the product of two irrational numbers will be rational.

Connection to Mathematics Standards

This FACT can be used to formatively assess students' understanding of any of the key ideas in mathematics. It also provides an opportunity to support any of the mathematical practices.

General Implementation Attributes

Ease of Use: Medium   **Time Demand:** Medium
Cognitive Demand: Medium

Modifications

Depending on the lesson and students' prior knowledge, sometimes *Success Indicators* can be developed with the students. *Success Indicators* are not fixed for a lesson and can change during the implementation of a lesson based on either difficulties students are having or finding out that a lesson isn't accomplishing what it was intended to do. Be aware that you may need to modify *Success Indicators* even after they are shared with students.

Caveats

Success Indicators are very useful for self- and peer assessment. However, you must still gather your own evidence of the extent to which students meet the criteria and not assume that students met the *Success Indicators* if they so indicated during self-assessment. Also, when writing *Success Indicators* in student-friendly language, be aware that sometimes the language used in standards is characteristic of the discipline of mathematics, and it is important for students to know and use that language rather than translate it into everyday language. Some *Success Indicators* should not be shared in advance if they reveal the answer to a task or activity. Share these *Success Indicators* after students have discovered the answer on their own.

Write *Success Indicators* that are aligned to the *Learning Intention* and include a balance of procedural and process indicators can be challenging. Working with a colleague or colleagues can be helpful. The *Bringing Math*

Students Into the Formative Assessment Equation (see the Appendix for more information) resource provides multiple planning templates and examples of *Learning Intentions* and *Success Indicators* (Creighton et al., 2015). The examples are targeted at the Grades 5–9 levels, but the majority of the planning resources and classroom materials are appropriate for the Grades 2–12 levels.

Use With Other Disciplines

This FACT can also be used in science, social studies, language arts, health, foreign language, and performing arts. For example, a lesson on the Sun–Earth connection to the seasons. The *Learning Intention* is "Understand what causes the seasons." The *Success Indicators* for this lesson are (1) I can describe Earth's tilt on its axis in relation to the sun at different times of the year, (2) I can use a model to show how Earth's tilted axis affects the angle of sunlight, (3) I can explain how the angle of sunlight affects seasonal temperatures, and (4) I can write a rebuttal to the argument that "the Earth is closer to the Sun in the summer, which is why it is warmer in the summertime."

My Notes

_____

_____

_____

_____

_____

FACT 43

SUCCESS INDICATOR
PROBLEM GENERATING

Description

Success Indicator Problem Generating is a technique that switches roles from the teacher as the generator of questions to the student as the question generator. The ability to formulate problems that show understanding of the ideas in the *Learning Intention* and *Success Indicators* can indicate the extent to which a student understands ideas that underlie the concept.

How This FACT Promotes Student Learning

When students are put in a position to develop problems related to the lesson's *Success Indicators*, they realize they have to draw on their own understanding of the topic. Generating good questions in mathematics requires more than superficial knowledge of the topic. It requires students to delve deeper into their existing knowledge base. As they formulate thinking questions, they practice metacognition by recognizing the level of understanding needed not only to form the question but also to respond to it.

How This FACT Informs Instruction

Success Indicator Problem Generating is used while instruction is still underway but after students' have had enough experience with the concept to have generalized ideas to use when generating problems. Teachers can also have students exchange or answer their own questions, revealing further information about students' ideas related to the topic. Selected student-generated questions can be saved and used at the end of a unit of instruction for self-assessment, reflection, or summative assessment.

Design and Administration

Refer to the *Success Indicators* for the lesson. Engage students in a whole-class discussion of the types of problems used so far in the lesson and how those problems allowed students to make progress toward meeting the one of the *Success Indicators*. Students work in pairs to develop two to three problems that, if solved correctly, would indicate that a student is on track to meeting the success indicator. For example, consider the following *Learning Intention* and *Success Indicators*:

Learning Intention: I will understand how to compare two decimals.

Success Indicator 1: I can use place value to name decimals.

Success Indicator 2: I can represent tenths and hundredths.

Success Indicator 3: I can explain why one decimal is greater than, less than, or equal to another.

After collecting evidence that students met *Success Indicators 1* and *2*, the teacher felt he did not have sufficient evidence to determine whether students were meeting *Success Indicator 3*. He decided to have students work in small groups to develop three problems that would provide evidence that students met *Success Indicator 3*. After developing the problems as a group, each group would present the problems to the class. The class would then solve them and discuss how each problem reflects the understanding in the *Success Indicator*. One group came up with the following questions:

1. Which is greater: 3.5 or 3.05? Explain why it is greater.

2. Arrange these numbers in order from least to greatest and tell why you listed them that way:

   1.0   0.6   1.25   1.09   1.3

3. Jared says 2.20 is the same amount as 2.2. Is Jared right or wrong?

The types of questions the students came up with and their answers provided evidence to the teacher on the extent to which students were meeting the success indicator.

Connection to Mathematics Standards

This FACT can be used to formatively assess students' understanding of any of the key mathematics ideas. It can be used to formatively assess how students use any of the mathematical practices.

General Implementation Attributes

Ease of Use: Medium   **Time Demand:** Medium
Cognitive Demand: Medium

Modifications

Students can work individually or in small groups to develop problems. This FACT can follow *Take Stock* (see FACT 44). *Success Indicator*

Problem Generating can also be used after a series of lessons as a review prior to a summative assessment such as a mid-unit test.

Caveats

Having students generate problems related to the *Success Indicators* too soon in the instructional cycle typically results in limited problem sets that are too similar to only the problems students have seen previously.

Use With Other Disciplines

This FACT is specific to problem solving in mathematics.

My Notes

_____

_____

_____

_____

_____

FACT 44

TAKE STOCK

Description

Take Stock (Creighton et al., 2015) is a way to model for students how they can reflect on their learning in relation to the *Learning Intention* and *Success Indicators*. In this strategy, students revisit the *Success Indicators* after the completion of a task or activity so they can summarize and share how their learning from the task relates to the learning goal.

How This FACT Promotes Student Learning

This FACT focuses students' attention on the relationship between the lesson activities and the *Success Indicators*. Seeing this relationship is an important element of students eventually learning to self-assess their work. Being explicit with students that you want them to learn to "take stock" of their own work, in the same way you are doing together, helps them develop self-regulation skills.

How This FACT Informs Instruction

The discussions that result from *Take Stock* can provide information about how clear to students the relationship is between what they've done in class and what they are supposed to be learning. This discussion helps establish a classroom culture in which pausing to consolidate your learning is considered an important and worthwhile learning activity.

Design and Administration

After the completion of a task or activity, engage students in a discussion that models a reflection on their learning. A sample structure for this discussion is as follows:

- "Who can describe for me what we've done so far with (this math task)?"

- "So in our success indicator (SI), we said we would (reread SI to students). Can someone else describe what this means in their own words?"

- **or** (Provide your own explanation relating it to what they've just done in class.)

- "In what way did this task help us work toward meeting the success indicator?"

This FACT can be quite effective when used in the middle of a lesson, as well as at the end of a lesson. Keep a running list next to the *Success Indicator* of important ideas or key terms that come up in the discussion. Repeat after the completion of additional tasks or activities, using the questions above. End with a final question: "Here are some ideas we listed from previous activities (review the list). In what way did this task help us work toward meeting the success indicator?"

The following vignette, adapted from Creighton et al. (2015) shows how this FACT is used to focus students on the success indicator, "I can explain how the variables, numbers, and operations in the equations represent the word problems." The problem they are working on is the following: At an online music site you can download an entire album for $12, and individual songs are $1.25 each. Jake has an e-music gift card for $25. If he buys one album, how many additional single songs can he buy? (1) What should the variable represent in this problem? (2) Write an algebraic equation that could be used to help you solve this problem.

Mr. C: So let's take a look at the second success indicator. Turn to your partner and talk for 30 seconds about how you would explain how the variables, numbers, and operations in the equations represent the word problems. Then write down what you think would be a strong response for this success indicator. Put your names on the back of your paper, please.

Using their responses, Mr. C takes stock of what the class understands. After the students have talked and written their responses, he collects the papers and randomly selects three to read. This time, he chooses a few papers randomly; other times, he chooses papers of specific students who he considers representative samples of the rest of the class. He sees that students can explain how the variable is represented in the word problem but are not solid on explaining the operations. From the information gathered, he gives them whole-class feedback:

Mr. C: I've only looked at the work from three pairs so far, and in those three, I'm seeing that they all have strong explanations of how the variables relate to the word problem. (He lines them up under the document camera so students can see all three responses, and he points out what it is about them that meets the success criterion.) I'm also noticing that the explanation of how the operations relate to the word problem seems to be where you're struggling a bit. (Finally, he uses the opportunity to clarify the *Learning Intention* and the success indicator.) Can anybody share one way that they think they've been explaining how the operations in the equations represent the word problem?

Ja'laine: You have to multiply, and you have to add.

Mr. C: So you're saying you need two different operations. How do you know that?

Ja'laine: Because you need to multiply $1.25 times the songs to find out what he spends on songs. Then you add it to the $12 to get $25 total.

Luis: And you have to subtract.

Mr. C: Why do you have to subtract?

Luis: Because you subtract $12 from $25, and that's how much money he can use to buy songs.

Mr. C: (Seeing an opportunity to use each student's comment to help clarify the success indicator.) So Ja'laine did a nice job explaining how the multiplication and addition were needed to set up the equation. That's what we're looking for in this success indicator—think about how the operations fit in the equation that you're creating to represent the problem. Luis went the next step beyond and correctly told us that you could subtract as part of solving the equation, but that's part of taking the next step to solve it and isn't part of this particular success criterion. So, Luis, you actually went beyond this success indicator.

Connection to Mathematics Standards

This FACT can be used to formatively assess students' understanding of any of the key ideas in mathematics. Depending on the mathematical practices included in the *Success Indicators*, it can be used with any of the mathematical practices.

General Implementation Attributes

Ease of Use: Medium   **Time Demand:** Medium
Cognitive Demand: Depends on problem

Modifications

Take Stock does not need to be limited only to use with a whole class. You can also refer to the running list of ideas and key terms when working with individuals, pairs, or groups of students.

Caveats

Be aware that some students may not know what taking stock means. The first few times you use this strategy, explain that we call this "taking stock of our learning" because we are going to reflect back on what we did and how it helped us. Use the analogy of stores taking stock of their inventory to help students understand this strategy. Stores take stock of their inventory to determine how their business is doing—what they've sold, how much inventory they have, and what new items they need to stock their shelves for the coming days.

Use With Other Disciplines

This FACT can also be used in science, social studies, language arts, health, foreign languages, and visual and performing arts. For example, in foreign language teachers can use this FACT to address the *Success Indicator*: I can conjugate regular verbs in the present tense.

My Notes

_____

_____

_____

_____

_____

FACT 45

TALK MOVES

Description

Facilitating meaningful mathematical discourse is one of the eight mathematics teaching practices in *Principles to Action* (National Council of Teachers of Mathematics, 2014). *Talk Moves* are verbal prompts used to help orchestrate such mathematics discussions. Different *Talk Moves* have different purposes, but they all serve to guide and facilitate mathematics discussions so they are more productive in revealing student thinking.

How This FACT Promotes Student Learning

Talk Moves support student learning in a variety of ways. They motivate students to participate in discussions and encourage students to listen carefully to their peers' ideas. They help support students in using evidence-based reasoning. Sometimes they encourage students to dig deeper into their own ideas and ways of thinking. They are strategically used during different points in a discussion to get students to think, reason, and build off the ideas of others in a safe and academically enriching learning environment. *Talk Moves* support language literacy skills such as the use of academic vocabulary, ways of speaking mathematically, and listening skills.

How This FACT Informs Instruction

By using this FACT the teacher gains a window into students' thinking that might not otherwise be visible, if a mathematics discussion had not been carefully orchestrated using *Talk Moves*. As students share their ideas, *Talk Moves* are used to probe deeper, thus revealing students' understandings or misconceptions. This information is then used to design or modify instruction that encourages the development of new ideas or builds on or challenges students' existing ideas and understandings.

Design and Administration

Before using *Talk Moves*, it is important to establish a classroom culture where students feel safe in expressing their ideas and everyone is accountable for each other's learning. One of the ways to do this is to establish norms or ground rules in advance and to enforce them until they become internalized by the students. *Talk Moves* can be used in pair discussions, small-group talk, or whole-class discussions. Begin by becoming familiar with the different *Talk Moves* and their purpose. Practice constructing some key questions in advance that incorporate different moves. Try out one or two moves at first until you are comfortable with them and then add another. When first using *Talk Moves*, refer to a copy of the different moves on a clipboard until you have internalized them well. The clipboard is also used to record ideas students express as you use the moves. These ideas are then addressed in subsequent instruction. Following are six *Talk Moves*, adapted from *Ready-Set-Science* (Michaels, Shouse, & Schweingruber, 2008), which you can use to facilitate productive mathematics discussions.

Revoicing. Sometimes it is difficult to understand what the student is trying to say when they struggle to put their thoughts into words. If you, as the teacher, have difficulty understanding what the student is saying, then the students who are listening are apt to have even greater difficulty. Clarity in expressing ideas is often needed when encouraging young students to share their thinking. Therefore, this *Talk Move* not only helps the student clarify his or her thinking; it provides clarity for the listeners as well, both the teacher and the students. By revoicing the student's idea as a question, the teacher is giving the student more think time to clarify his or her ideas. It is also a way to make sure the student's idea is accessible to the other students who are listening and following the discussion.

Restating Someone Else's Reasoning. While the preceding *Talk Move* (revoicing) is a move used by the teacher and a student, this move has other students reword or repeat what a student shares during a discussion. It should then be followed up with the student whose idea was repeated or reworded. The benefit to using this *Talk Move* during discussions about mathematics ideas is that it gives the class more think time and opportunity to process each student's contribution to the math talk. It also provides another version of the explanation, which may be an easier version for some students to understand. This *Talk Move* is especially useful with ELLs. It encourages language use and development while simultaneously providing the teacher with a clarification of what the student is thinking. Additionally, it acknowledges to the students that the teacher, as well as the students in the class, are listening to each other.

Asking Students to Apply Their Own Reasoning to Someone Else's Reasoning. In the mathematics class, students are encouraged to make a conjecture and share the reasoning that supports their conjecture. This *Talk Move* is used with a variety of formative assessment probes and elicitation/ prediction questions, to make sure students have had time to evaluate a claim made by another student and the reasoning used to support the claim. It helps students zero in and focus on the reasoning their peers use. Note that the teacher is not asking the other students whether they merely agree or disagree with someone's claim; they also have to explain why. This *Talk Move* helps students compare their thinking to someone else's, and in the process it helps them be more explicit in their own reasoning.

Prompting Students for Further Participation. After bringing to the surface and clarifying the different ideas that emerge during a discussion, the teacher prompts others in the class to contribute by agreeing, disagreeing, or adding on to what was already shared. This *Talk Move* encourages all students to evaluate the strength of each other's arguments. It promotes equitable and accountable discussion in which everyone is expected to take part.

Asking Students to Explicate Their Reasoning. This *Talk Move* encourages students to go deeper with their reasoning and be more explicit in their explanations. It helps them focus on the evidence that best supports their conjecture and build on the reasoning of others.

Using Wait Time. This is actually a silent move rather than a *Talk Move*. One of the hardest things for teachers to do during a discussion is refrain from commenting immediately on students' responses. There are two types of wait time that should be used during math talk. The first is for the teacher to wait at least 5 seconds after posing a question so the students have adequate think time. The second is for the teacher, as well as the students, to practice waiting at least 5 seconds before commenting on a student's response. This strategy is especially important to use with ELLs, as well as students who may be shy or reluctant to contribute ideas in front of the whole class. By waiting, even though silence can be difficult for the teacher, this strategy supports students' thinking and reasoning, by providing more time for them to construct an explanation or evaluate the arguments of others. It provides greater inclusivity for all students in the class to participate in productive math talk by acknowledging the time they need to think through their ideas.

Talk Moves can be used to orchestrate discussions around students' ideas related to various assessment probes, such as the ones in the *Uncovering Student Thinking* series (see the Appendix). Figure 3.40 shows how the six productive *Talk Moves* are used with the mathematics formative assessment probe in Figure 3.39.

Connection to Mathematics Standards

Talk Moves can be used with any of the key mathematics ideas. This FACT can be used to support any of the mathematical practices. It is especially useful in helping students construct arguments and evaluate their reasoning.

General Implementation Attributes

Ease of Use: Medium   **Time Demand:** Medium
Cognitive Demand: Medium

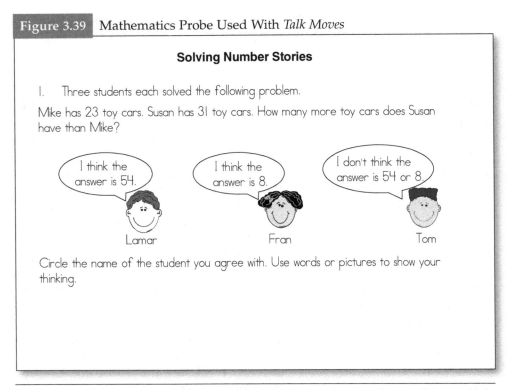

Figure 3.39   Mathematics Probe Used With *Talk Moves*

Solving Number Stories

1.   Three students each solved the following problem.

Mike has 23 toy cars. Susan has 31 toy cars. How many more toy cars does Susan have than Mike?

> I think the answer is 54.

Lamar

> I think the answer is 8.

Fran

> I don't think the answer is 54 or 8.

Tom

Circle the name of the student you agree with. Use words or pictures to show your thinking.

Source: Tobey, C. R., & Fagan, E. (2013). *Uncovering student thinking about mathematics in the Common Core, grades K–2: 20 formative assessment probes* (p. 123). Thousand Oaks, CA: Corwin. Used with permission.

Modifications

Talk Moves are used not only by the teacher. Students can also be encouraged to use *Talk Moves* with each other when engaged in pair or small-group discussions. Provide students with examples of *Talk Moves* they can use with each other and practice using them in math discussions.

Caveats

Be aware that it takes time to build a classroom where rich, respectful, productive discussions are the norm. It is important to establish a culture of respectful and productive talk to use this FACT successfully. This is best done at the beginning of the school year, by setting expectations and ground rules that everyone agrees to abide by.

Use With Other Disciplines

This FACT can also be used in science, social studies, language arts, health, foreign languages, and visual and performing arts. For example, *Talk Moves* can be used in social studies when discussing current issues.

Figure 3.40 *Talk Moves* With Formative Assessment Probes

Talk Move	Example of Using the Talk Move With a Formative Assessment Probe
Revoicing	"So let me see if I understand the reason for your answer choice." "You're agreeing with Fran because _____?" "Let me see if I understand, you are saying _____?"
Asking students to restate someone else's reasoning	"Can you repeat in your own words what Latisha's explanation is? Is that right, Latisha? Is that what you said?" "Who can restate Freddie's rule in their own words?"
Asking students to apply their own reasoning to someone else's reasoning	"Do you agree or disagree with Emma's reason for choosing Fran as the best answer? What is your reasoning?" "Can you tell us why you agree with what Sam said? What is your reasoning for choosing Fran instead of Lamar?"
Prompting students for further participation	"Would someone like to add on to the reasons why some of you chose Fran as the person you most agree with in the probe?" "Does someone have another way to solve the problem?" "What do others think about the ideas we have shared so far. Do you agree or disagree?"
Asking students to explicate their reasoning	"Why isn't Lamar the best answer?" "What does 'how many more' tell you about this problem?" "Say more about that."
Using wait time	"Take your time. We'll wait." "I want everyone to think first and then I will ask you to share your thinking about the best answer."

My Notes

_____

_____

_____

_____

_____

FACT 46

THERMOMETER FEEDBACK

Description

Thermometer Feedback provides a quick, visual nonverbal feedback check after completing a task. The students hold their hands up at different levels according to a scale established by the teacher that indicates how well they think they did on the task.

How This FACT Promotes Student Learning

Thermometer Feedback promotes metacognition and helps students develop self-assessment skills. By raising their hands to a level that indicates how well they thought they completed a task, students have an opportunity to reflect and self-assess.

How This FACT Informs Instruction

Thermometer Feedback provides a quick opportunity for teachers to find out how well students think they did after completing a task but before the task is turned in. If the students' feedback is warm or hot, the teacher can collect the work to examine and provide feedback as needed. If the students' feedback is cool or cold, it is an indication that the work is not ready to be turned in and that additional instruction is needed for students to complete the task so that feedback can be used successfully. It may also indicate students who need individual assistance.

Design and Administration

After completing a task, have students imagine a thermometer. If their hand is held all the way up, the temperature on the thermometer is hot. Hot means "I think I did very well." If their hand is held by their shoulder, it indicates cold, meaning "I did not do well. I need help." If their hand is held halfway up, it is warm, meaning, "I did OK but could do better." For example, after completing a task to explain to the public what their chance is of winning their state's lottery if they buy a single ticket, the teacher says, "Please hold your hands up to indicate how well you think you did on preparing a public message to explain to buyers of a lottery ticket what their chance of winning is. Hot means you think you did an excellent job and your probability is accurate." (The teacher holds an arm straight up.) "Warm means you did a good job but may improve on some parts of your explanation or calculation." (The teacher holds an arm halfway up.) "Cold means you had difficulty and need help figuring this out or explaining it." (The teacher holds an arm up with hand by shoulder.)

Connection to Mathematics Standards

Thermometer Feedback can be used with any of the key mathematics ideas. This FACT is most effective in providing feedback on the mathematical practice of solving problems and persevering in solving them.

General Implementation Attributes

Ease of Use: High   **Time Demand:** Low   **Cognitive Demand:** Low

Modifications

A classroom poster of a thermometer can be labeled with feedback levels for students to refer to when giving feedback. An image of a thermometer can also be posted and students can attach sticky notes onto the levels of the thermometer, indicating their feedback. For cool or cold feedback, students can write on their sticky note what they need for help.

Caveats

Be aware this is self-reported data. It should be followed up with an examination of the students' completed tasks even if students indicate warm and hot feedback.

Use With Other Disciplines

This FACT can also be used in science, social studies, language arts, health, foreign languages, and visual and performing arts. For example, students can give feedback on how well they think they executed a dance move in performing arts.

My Notes

_____

_____

_____

_____

_____

FACT 47

TRAFFIC LIGHT SLIDERS

Description

The *Traffic Light Sliders* FACT is similar to the *Traffic Light Cards* FACT (Keeley & Tobey, 2011). It is a variation of "traffic lighting" that uses three physical "indicator lights" to visually show the extent to which elementary students can undertake a learning task or activity in relation to a learning goal. The sliders are placed on the desk and used as a visual indicator for monitoring purposes as the students are working on a task. The teacher circulates among the students, checking which students need help and which students are able to proceed on their own with the task. For example, the green light can be used to signal "I can do this on my own without help." The yellow can be used to indicate "I can do most of this on my own, but I need some help." The red can be used to indicate "I am having difficulty and need help."

How This FACT Promotes Student Learning

Traffic Light Sliders encourage students to take ownership of their learning. By setting the marker to green, yellow, or red, students monitor their own ability to complete an assigned task with understanding. Because understanding can change during completion of a task, this FACT gives students an opportunity to change their indicator color at any time during a lesson.

How This FACT Informs Instruction

Used as a monitoring strategy, this FACT visually helps teachers gauge how students are proceeding with an assigned task. It enables teachers to make quick assessments of the entire class by observing which students signal a need for assistance or which students can proceed independently with the task. For example, if the teacher observes that most of the class has their sliders pointed to the red light, this is an indication to stop and provide assistance or further instruction to the entire class. If there is a mix of red, yellow, and green light indicators, the teacher can provide assistance first to the students who need it the most (red), followed by the yellows, and then check in with the greens. The traffic light indicators can also be used to group students for feedback and assistance. Students with green lights can be asked to pair up with the yellow-light students to provide peer assistance and feedback while the teacher works with the red-light students. This FACT can be combined with *Learning Intentions* (FACT 23) and *Success Indicators* (FACT 42). The sliders can also be used with *Confidence Level Assessment* (FACT 3), particularly when students are engaged in a task that has them apply or practice what they have been learning (Wiliam, 2011). For example, green may indicate "I feel confident doing this on my own," yellow may indicate "I feel confident that I can do most of this on my own," and red may indicate "I don't feel confident doing this on my own. Please check in with me."

Design and Administration

Figure 3.41 shows a photograph of a traffic light slider. Print a traffic light graphic, in color, on half a sheet of 8.5- × 11-inch card stock (traffic light graphics can be found in many clip art collections, including free clip art at www.freeclipartnow.com). Cut two parallel slits, an inch apart, to the left of the traffic light graphic. Cut two matching arrows from card stock. The arrows should be about 3 inches long. Slip one arrow underneath the slits with the end and the pointer on top of the paper. Place the other arrow on top of the paper, matched up to the arrow underneath it. Staple the arrows together at the pointer and the end of the arrow so the staples are on opposite sides of the slits. The arrow should now be able to slide up and down, pointing to the red, yellow, or green light.

| Figure 3.41 | *Traffic Light Slider* |

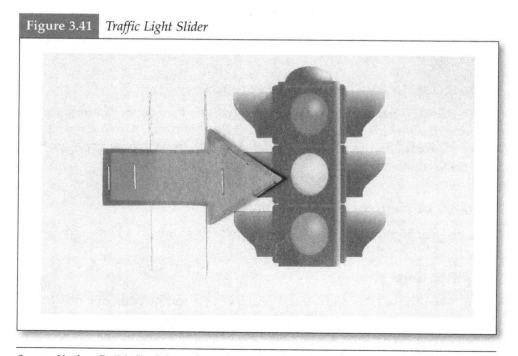

This FACT is best used with elementary students and is most effective when combined with *Learning Intentions* and *Success Indicators*. Provide each student with a slider to place on a corner of his or her desk or workspace so it is visible to the teacher. At the beginning of the lesson, when the teacher shares the *Learning Intention* and *Success Indicators* for the day's lesson, have students move their sliders to indicate the extent to which they are clear on the purpose of the lesson and what they need to do to provide evidence of their learning. A scan helps the teacher determine how clear the purpose of the lesson is and whether students know what the expected outcomes are regarding what they can do to show evidence of meeting the learning target.

As students work on the task or activity, ask them to adjust their pointer at any time to indicate how well they are moving toward the *Learning Intention*. For example, second-grade students might be working on a bar graph for the *Learning Intention*: I understand how to display my data on a bar graph. The students take the data from their class activity of finding out what pets students have and how many of each type and create a bar graph. Some students may have difficulty in setting up their graph. They move their sliders to red. One student is proceeding with the task but wonders if she should color the bars different colors or just use one color. She moves her pointer to yellow and keeps working on her graph until the teacher can assist her. While the students are working on the task, the teacher can use these visual clues to determine when to modify instruction for the entire class or address individual student's learning related to making a graph of one's data.

Connection to Mathematics Standards

This FACT can be used to formatively assess students' understanding of any of the key ideas in mathematics. It is most useful when students are using the mathematics practice of making sense of problems and persevering in solving them.

General Implementation Attributes

Ease of Use: High   **Time Demand:** Low   **Cognitive Demand:** Low

Modifications

In addition to the individual sliders, you might consider creating a traffic light poster for the class to remind them what each color light signifies for the activity they are engaged in. For example, a poster on levels of understanding of a task might include Green—I understand what I am doing and can explain it to someone else, Yellow—I mostly understand what I am doing but may need some help, and Red—I do not understand what I am doing and need help. You might use several different posters for different indicators depending on your purpose for using the traffic light sliders (e.g., confidence levels, readiness to proceed, levels of interest). This FACT can also be used in group work to signal the group's ability to proceed with the task.

Caveats

Be aware this is self-reported information that may be more or less reliable, depending on your students' willingness to indicate their ability to proceed with a task on their own. Be sure to model this the first time with young students. Students must remember to reset their green pointer when they may need help or are stuck on a task.

Use With Other Disciplines

This FACT can also be used in science, social studies, language arts, health, foreign languages, and visual and performing arts for any type of individual or group activity. For example, in a language arts class students might use a *Traffic Light Slider* when making a flip book.

My Notes

_____

_____

_____

_____

_____

FACT 48

VDR (VOTE, DISCUSS, REVOTE)

Description

Vote, Discuss, Revote (VDR) begins with an elicitation question in which students vote on an answer choice. After the votes are tallied, students discuss their answer choice in pairs, then in a small group, and, finally, in the whole group. After discussion a revote is taken, allowing students to change their answer choice based on new information and the compelling arguments of others. Tallies are shared with students to document how the class ideas are changing. Discussion and revoting can be repeated several times to see if the class is moving toward consensus.

How This FACT Promotes Student Learning

VDR begins with an elicitation question that provides an opportunity for all students to share their ideas by voting on the answer that best matches their thinking. This helps students recognize that not everyone thinks the same way initially and that learning is a process of first uncovering thinking and then working through ideas. After seeing the range of answer choices in the class, students have opportunities to share their thinking with others, explicate their reasoning, and reorganize and modify their thinking as they evaluate the arguments of others. Talking through one's ideas provides an opportunity to revise, clarify, or organize one's thinking. Revoting provides an opportunity for students to recognize how the class ideas are changing and compare the results to their own thinking.

How This FACT Informs Instruction

During the voting process, the teacher is able to gather data quickly on different ideas held by the students. As students engage in discussion, the teacher circulates and listens for evidence of understanding or misconceptions and makes note of students who present strong arguments using mathematical ideas. The revote provides an opportunity to see if students changed their thinking based on compelling arguments of others, both mathematically correct and incorrect. As the revote data come closer to the best answer, the teacher may ask particular students who chose the best answer and were able to support it with a strong mathematical argument to share their thinking with the whole class. As the whole class evaluates and provides feedback on the answer choices and selected arguments, the teacher listens and determines next steps for instruction, particularly for students whose ideas are very resistant to change through discussion.

Design and Administration

Select an assessment probe from the *Uncovering Student Thinking* series (see the Appendix) or create your own probing question to use as an elicitation. For the first part of this FACT, it is important that students work individually and not discuss their answer yet. Provide the stimulus question and ask students to commit to an answer choice that best matches their thinking. Provide time for them to think and record some ideas or calculations that support their answer choice. When students are ready, take a class vote using a show of hands (or anonymous strategies if students are not yet ready to publicly share their thinking) for each answer choice. Count the responses for each answer choice and record the tallies so students can see the results.

Now ask students to share and discuss their answer choice with a partner. If they chose the same answer, have them discuss and formulate an argument about why that is the best answer. If their answer choices differ, have them engage in a discussion, presenting their best argument to support their answer choice. Encourage students to ask further questions of each other, if needed, to clarify their ideas. Circulate and listen to the discussions, making note of students with evidence of understanding who can present a strong argument, as well as students who reveal misunderstandings. Then take a revote. Tally the votes and record next to the previous votes so students (and the teacher) can see if ideas are changing. Repeat this process in small groups.

After the small-group revote, ask for some volunteers to share their best thinking with the whole class. Be sure to have at least one student who demonstrated understanding and could provide a solid argument, share their thinking with the whole class. Allow an opportunity for other students to evaluate, give feedback, or provide rebuttals. After the whole-class discussion, provide another opportunity to revote. Tally the new results, post, and compare the difference. If most of the class has moved toward the best answer, discuss with the whole class why it is the best answer, using evidence from students' strong arguments as well as bringing in new information to guide their thinking. If students are stuck and are not moving toward the correct answer, consider next steps for instruction that will address students' misunderstandings and guide them toward the best answer and explanation. Then revisit the probe or question again and take a final revote, followed by a teacher-guided class discussion on the best answer and explanation.

The following vignette describes how a teacher used *VDR*:

After giving his students the Parallelogram probe in Figure 3.42 and learning that his students were making visual assumptions rather than the given information to determine if a figure is a parallelogram, the teacher developed a series of computer-based

Figure 3.42   Example of an Assessment Probe Used With *VDR*

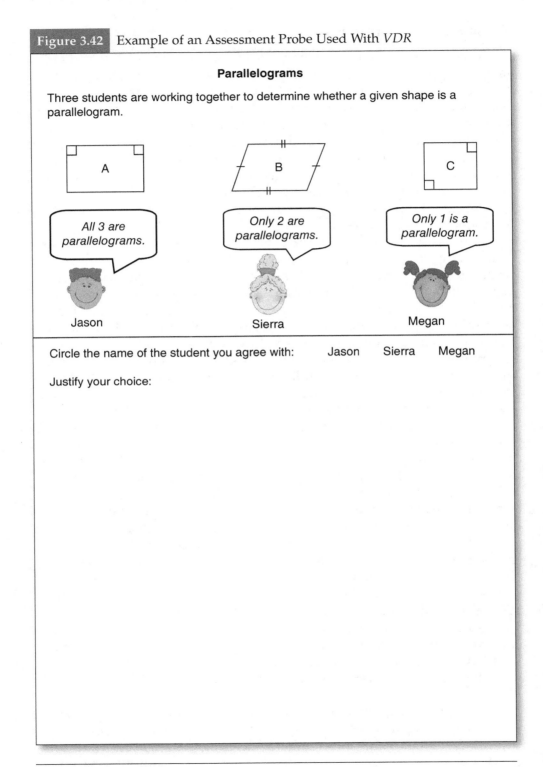

investigations that would allow his students to determine the list of minimal requirements needed to prove a quadrilateral is a parallelogram. He introduced the *Learning Intention* and *Success Indicators* to launch the 2-day lesson.

Today's Learning Intention: Understand the minimal number of conditions necessary to ensure a quadrilateral is a parallelogram.

Success Indicators:

- I can describe the minimum conditions.
- I can explain or show why one of these conditions are needed.
- I can use the conditions to determine if a quadrilateral is a parallelogram.

Periodically, the teacher stopped the class to *Take Stock* (FACT 44) by capturing what the students had learned from the investigations. As student pairs suggested a possible minimal requirement, he listed the idea posted on a chart. After collecting three ideas, he asked students to vote on each idea (yes—minimal requirement; no—not a minimal requirement as written). For ideas with yes and no votes, he asked for clarification from several students and then gave the pairs additional time to investigate. At the beginning of the next round, he had the students revote on the previous listed ideas before using further discussion to add clarifying language to existing ideas as well as adding new ideas to vote on. With each round, the teacher could see that the class was moving toward the correct language of minimal requirements listed, based on listening to and evaluating the arguments of others. He also knew there was one missing minimal requirement to address now that the *VDR* was completed.

Connection to Mathematics Standards

This FACT can be used to formatively assess students' understanding of any of the key ideas in mathematics. It also provides an opportunity to use any of the mathematics practices, especially constructing viable arguments.

General Implementation Attributes

Ease of Use: High   **Time Demand:** Low   **Cognitive Demand:** Medium

Modifications

VDR can be used with anonymous response strategies if peer pressure affects voting for an answer choice. Strategies such as *Fingers Under Chin* (FACT 14) is a way in which the voting phase of this FACT can be kept anonymous.

Caveats

Make sure you choose a question about which it is likely that students will have a range of different answers and explanations. It is important to establish discussion norms prior to using this FACT so students engage in respectful and productive discussion.

Use With Other Disciplines

This FACT can also be used in science, social studies, language arts, health, foreign languages, and visual and performing arts. For example, *VDR* can be used in social studies to debate social issues, such as "Should the death penalty be abolished?" As the teacher listens to the debate and monitors changes in students' beliefs, he or she can gather evidence of students' understanding of political, social, legal, and ethical implications.

My Notes

_____

_____

_____

_____

_____

FACT 49

WHAT STUCK WITH YOU TODAY?

Description

What Stuck With You Today? is a metacognitive strategy used to help students connect with the important goals of a lesson. Students reflect on the lesson and identify the key point or points that show they are making progress toward meeting the *Success Indicators*.

How This FACT Promotes Student Learning

Having students answer the question *What Stuck With You Today?* provides an opportunity for students to reflect upon their progress and to become aware of what they think enabled their learning. Rather than just rating how well they are meeting each success indicator, this reflection FACT focuses the student's attention on the concepts, ideas, or strategies that helped them meet the success indicator(s). Teachers often use quick checks such as *Thumbs Up, Down, and Sideways* with few follow-up opportunities for students to think about what helped them meet the learning goal. This FACT helps students become more aware of how their own learning needs in mathematics can be met.

How This FACT Informs Instruction

This FACT is used at the end of a lesson to gather information on what students feel was the most significant idea or ideas that stuck. Teachers can quickly administer, collect, and sort responses to make judgments about how well the key ideas of the lesson were perceived as important by the students. If the responses of the students differ from the important points the lesson was intended to develop, the teacher can use this information to clarify and add more emphasis to those key points.

Design and Administration

At the end of a lesson, ask students to describe orally or in writing what stuck with them related to the *Learning Intention* and *Success Indicators* of the lesson. For example, a lesson on linear measurement might conclude with "Today we investigated and discussed different types of graphs that can be used to represent categorical data. What stuck with you that best helps you understand the similarities and differences between these types of graphs?" Collect and analyze students' responses to decide if the lesson met its goal or needs to be modified. Be sure to let students know how you used their responses. When they understand that the information is seriously considered by you to make changes that will benefit them, they will respond thoughtfully and in detail.

Connection to Mathematics Standards

This FACT can be used to formatively assess students' understanding of any of the mathematics key ideas. Depending on the goals for the lesson, it provides an opportunity to see if students recognize the use of any of the mathematical practices.

General Implementation Attributes

Ease of Use: High   **Time Demand:** Low   **Cognitive Demand:** Medium

Modifications

The prompt for *What Stuck With You Today?* is not limited to only content learning. It can also be used with classroom practices such as giving and receiving feedback or engaging in mathematical discourse.

Caveats

Learning Intentions and *Success Indicators* often span more than one class period. Use *What Stuck With You Today?* after students have had sufficient opportunity to experience the activity or goal of the lesson.

Use With Other Disciplines

This FACT can also be used in science, social studies, language arts, health, foreign languages, and visual and performing arts. For example, in social studies teachers can use this FACT after students watch a video on the civil rights movement.

My Notes

FACT 50

X MARKS THE SPOT

Description

X Marks the Spot (Creighton et al., 2015) is a technique that engages students to self-assess their progress toward meeting the *Success Indicators* of a lesson-level learning target. Students place an X on a line to indicate the level success in meeting the *Success Indicator* at a given point in the lesson. In addition, students are asked to provide evidence for their self-assessment.

How This FACT Promotes Student Learning

X Marks the Spot provides a structured way for students to self-assess their learning against each of the *Success Indicators* for a lesson providing a process that students' can internalize and use independently. Learning to provide evidence to justify the self-assessment helps students move beyond generic explanations such as "I did all the problems." Use of language such as "not yet" and "getting close" within the rating scale supports a growth mindset.

How This FACT Informs Instruction

The FACT provides information both in terms of the content of the lesson as well as how well students are able to use the *Success Indicators* to gauge their level of success. If students' self-assessment is off-base, additional time can be spent with small groups or the whole class to build additional understanding of what it looks like and sounds like to meet a *Success Indicator* within a *Learning Intention*. Samples of student work, either actual or fictitious, can be shared and discussed regarding how the work does and doesn't yet meet the target.

Design and Administration

Make copies of the *X Marks the Spot* Template in Figure 3.43. Fill in the *Success Indicators* for the lesson, one in each row of the template, according to how many *Success Indicators* there are for the lesson. For example, after completing a lesson on ratios, the teacher may have them complete an *X Marks the Spot* reflection on the three *Success Indicators* for the 2-day lesson:

1. Use appropriate ratios for a given situation.

2. Use multiplication or division to compare ratios.

3. Explain why you can use ratios to compare quantities in more than one way.

| Figure 3.43 | *X Marks the Spot* Template |

Success Indicator	Self-Assessment			Evidence
	I am not there yet and need help.	I am getting closer and know what I need to do next.	I have met the indicator and can help others.	
	I am not there yet and need help.	I am getting closer and know what I need to do next.	I have met the indicator and can help others.	
	I am not there yet and need help.	I am getting closer and know what I need to do next.	I have met the indicator and can help others.	

Distribute the recording slip to each student. Students place an X on the line to indicate where they feel they fall with each success indicator. If students have indicated that they understand, they write a brief explanation in the Evidence column to support their claim. To help students know what to write in the Evidence column, a teacher might use one of the following prompts or something similar:

- Give an example from your work that shows you understand.
- What is one thing you did in your work that best shows your understanding? (e.g., "I wrote a clear explanation of the idea.")
- What could you do to show me you understand? (e.g., "I could explain two different ways to solve the problem," or "I could explain how ___ and ___ are related.")

Collect the students' recording slips and review them after class to inform the next day's instruction.

Connection to Mathematics Standards

This FACT can be used with any of the key mathematics ideas. Depending on the *Success Indicators* selected, it can be used to formatively assess any of the mathematical practices.

General Implementation Attributes

Ease of Use: Medium   **Time Demand:** Medium
Cognitive Demand: Medium

Modifications

After students have completed their reflection slip, designate a line (real or imaginary) along the floor that represents the self-assessment line on the template. For each *Success Indicator*, one at a time, ask students to stand along the line where they marked themselves. Have a brief whole-class discussion about where people are falling along the line and what is being most confusing at this point.

You can also bend the line as shown in Figure 3.44. When students have placed themselves along the line, find the midpoint of the line and have students "bend the line" at the midpoint so that each student is facing another student. This will place students with the most understanding facing students with the least understanding, and students with moderate understanding facing each other.

Caveats

Initially, as students are learning to use this FACT, they may need some guidance on what types of evidence show that they have met the success indicator.

Figure 3.44   Bending the Line

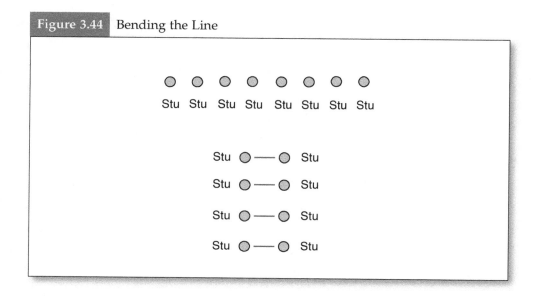

Use With Other Disciplines

This FACT can also be used in science, social studies, language arts, health, foreign languages, and visual and performing arts. For example, after completing a lesson on Amendments to the Constitution, students complete a reflection on two *Success Indicators* for the lesson.

My Notes

_____

_____

_____

_____

_____

Appendix

ANNOTATED RESOURCES FOR MATHEMATICS FORMATIVE ASSESSMENT

The resources listed below are referred to in Chapters 1–3. They provide additional material for you to use with the FACTs and to extend your learning about effective mathematics instruction and assessment.

Formative Assessment Probes in Mathematics. The *Uncovering Student Thinking in Mathematics* series is a collection of seven books (and still growing) and over 300 assessment probes that can be used from Kindergarten through college and for teacher professional development. Many of the examples used in Chapter 3 come from this series. The books are available through Corwin at www.corwin.com or through www.amazon.com. Descriptions of the books and the probes can be found on the website at www.uncoveringstudentideas.org.

Formative Assessment Probes in Science. The *Uncovering Student Ideas in Science* series is a collection of over 10 books (and still growing) and over 350 assessment probes that can be used from kindergarten through college and for teacher professional development. These are similar to the mathematics probes but focus on science concepts. Several of the books include probes that use mathematics in science. The books are available through NSTA Press at http://www.nsta.org/store or through www.amazon.com. Descriptions of the books and the probes can be found on the website at www.uncoveringstudentideas.org.

Learning Intentions, Success Indicators, and Feedback. While they may go by various names (learning targets, lesson objectives, success criteria, "I can" statements) additional information on setting learning goals for a lesson, indicators to help students and teachers monitor the extent to which students are moving toward conceptual understanding, and the feedback cycle are included in the following resources: *Embedded Formative*

Assessment (Wiliam, 2011); *Formative Assessment-Making It Happen in the Classroom* (Heritage, 2010); *Formative Assessment in the Secondary Classroom* (Clarke, 2005), and *Bringing Math Students into the Formative Assessment Equation* (Creighton, Tobey, Karnowski, & Fagan, 2015). This last book is available at the Corwin website at www.corwin.com.

Mathematics Formative Assessment: 75 Practical Strategies for Linking Assessment, Instruction, and Learning (Keeley & Tobey, 2011). This book is the first in this mathematics series (Volume 1). It is copublished with the National Council of Teachers of Mathematics (NCTM). It includes 75 FACTs and three chapters that can build your capacity to use mathematics formative assessment purposefully and effectively. It is highly recommended that you have a copy of Volume 1 because the material in Chapters 1 through 3 is not duplicated in this book. It is available through Corwin at www.corwin.com or through www.amazon.com.

Math Talk. An excellent book for learning how to orchestrate productive mathematics discourse is *Five Practices for Orchestrating Productive Mathematics Discussions* (Smith & Stein, 2011). This book is available through NCTM at www.nctm.org/store, Corwin at www.corwin.com, or through www.amazon.com. Another excellent resource is published by Math Solutions, *Classroom Discussions: Using Math Talk to Help Students Learn* (Chapin, O'Connor, & Anderson, 2009). This book is available through www.amazon.com. Googling the term mathematics discourse will also reveal several useful online resources.

Ranking Tasks. Ranking tasks are often used in physics to uncover misconceptions by probing students' thinking about variations in a set of objects or situations. An extensive set of ranking tasks is published in the book *Ranking Task Exercises in Physics* (O'Kuma et al., 2000) and is available through www.amazon.com.

Uncovering Student Ideas **Web Site and Social Media.** www.uncovering studentideas.org includes information, tools, and resources related to science and mathematics formative assessment. There are links to a Facebook site and Twitter associated with the author's (Page Keeley) work in formative assessment.

References

Ames, C. (1992). Classrooms: Goals, structures, and student motivation. *Journal of Educational Psychology, 84,* 261–271.

Black, P., Harrison, C., Lee, C., Marshall, B., & Wiliam, D. (2003). *Assessment for learning.* Berkshire, England: Open University Press.

Chapin, S. H., O'Connor, M. C., & Anderson, N. C. (2003). *Classroom discussions: Using math talk to help students learn, grades 1–6.* Sausalito, CA: Math Solutions Publications.

Clarke, S. (2005). *Formative assessment in the secondary classroom.* London, England: Hodder Murray.

Cohen, E. (1994). *Designing groupwork: Strategies for the heterogeneous classroom.* New York, NY: Teachers College Press.

Council of Chief State School Officers. (2008). Attributes of effective formative assessment. Retrieved from http://www.ccsso.org/Documents/2008/Attributes_of_Effective_2008.pdf

Council of Chief State School Officers. (2010). Implementing the Common Core State Standards. Retrieved from http://corestandards.org

Creighton, S. J., Tobey, C. R., Karnowski, E., & Fagan, E. (2015). *Bringing math students into the formative assessment equation: Tools and strategies for the middle grades.* Thousand Oaks, CA: Corwin.

de Bono, E. (1994). *De Bono's thinking course.* New York, NY: Facts on File.

Fennema, E., & Romberg, T. (1999). *Mathematics classrooms that promote understanding.* London, England: Psychology Press.

Frayer, D. A., Frederick, W. C., & Klausmeier, H. G. (1969). *A schema for testing the level of concept mastery: Report from the Project on Situational Variables and Efficiency of Concept Learning* (Report No. 16). Madison: University of Wisconsin, Wisconsin Research and Development Center for Cognitive Learning.

Harlen, W. (2007). Criteria for evaluating systems for student assessment. *Studies in Educational Evaluation, 33*(1), 15–28.

Hattie, J., & Timperley, H. (2007). The power of feedback. *Review of Educational Research, 77,* 81–112.

Heritage, M. (2010). *Formative assessment: Making it happen in the classroom.* Thousand Oaks, CA: Corwin.

Hudgins, D., Prather, E., Grayson, D., & Smits, D. (2006). Effectiveness of collaborative ranking tasks on student understanding of key astronomy concepts. *Astronomy Education Review, 5*(1), 1–22.

Karp, K., Bush, S., & Dougherty, B. (2014). 13 rules that expire. *Teaching Children Mathematics, 21*, 18–25.

Keeley, P. (2008). *Science formative assessment: 75 practical strategies linking assessment, instruction, and learning.* Thousand Oaks, CA: Corwin.

Keeley, P. (2015). *Science formative assessment, volume 2: 50 more practical strategies linking assessment, instruction, and learning.* Thousand Oaks, CA: Corwin.

Keeley, P. (2016). *Science formative assessment, volume 1: 75 practical strategies linking assessment, instruction, and learning* (2nd ed.). Thousand Oaks, CA: Corwin.

Keeley, P., & Rose, C. (2006). *Mathematics curriculum: Bridging the gap between standards and practice.* Thousand Oaks, CA: Corwin.

Keeley, P., & Tobey, C. (2011). *Mathematics formative assessment, volume 1: 75 practical strategies linking assessment, instruction, and learning.* Thousand Oaks, CA: Corwin.

Leahy, S., Lyon, C., Thompson, M., & Wiliam, D. (2005). Classroom assessment: Minute-by-minute and day-by-day. *Educational Leadership, 63*(3), 18–24.

Maloney, D. (1987). Ranking tasks: A new kind of test item. *Journal of College Science Teaching, 16*(6), 510–514.

Michaels, S., Shouse, A., & Schweingruber, H. (2008). *Ready, set, science: Putting research to work in K–8 classrooms.* Washington, DC: National Academy Press.

Mundry, S., Keeley, P., & Tobey, C. R. (2012). *Facilitator's guide to mathematics curriculum topic study.* Thousand Oaks, CA: Corwin.

National Council of Teachers of Mathematics. (2014). *Principles to actions: Ensuring mathematical success for all.* Reston, VA: Author.

Naylor, S., Keogh, B., & Goldsworthy, A. (2004). *Active assessment: Thinking and learning in science.* London, England: David Fulton.

O'Kuma, T, Maloney, D., & Hieggelke, C. (2000). *Ranking task exercises in physics.* Upper Saddle River, NJ: Prentice Hall.

Rose, C. M., Minton, L., & Arline, C. (2007). *Uncovering student thinking in mathematics: 25 formative assessment probes.* Thousand Oaks, CA: Corwin.

Sadler, D. R. (1989). Formative assessment and the design of instructional systems. *Instructional Science, 18*, 119–140.

Siegler, R. (1976). Three aspects of cognitive development. *Cognitive Psychology, 8*, 481–520.

Smith, M. S., & Stein, M. K. (2011). *Five practices for orchestrating productive mathematics discussions.* Thousand Oaks, CA: Corwin.

Tobey, C. R., & Arline, C. (2009). *Uncovering student thinking in mathematics, grades 6–12: 30 formative assessment probes for the secondary classroom.* Thousand Oaks, CA: Corwin.

Tobey, C. R., & Arline, C. (2014a). *Uncovering student thinking about mathematics in the Common Core, grades 6–8: 25 formative assessment probes.* Thousand Oaks, CA: Corwin.

Tobey, C. R., & Arline, C. (2014b). *Uncovering student thinking about mathematics in the Common Core, high school: 25 formative assessment probes.* Thousand Oaks, CA: Corwin.

Tobey, C. R., & Fagan, E. (2013). *Uncovering student thinking about mathematics in the Common Core, grades K–2: 20 formative assessment probes.* Thousand Oaks, CA: Corwin.

Tobey, C. R., & Fagan, E. (2014). *Uncovering student thinking about mathematics in the Common Core, grades 3–5: 25 formative assessment probes.* Thousand Oaks, CA: Corwin.

Tobey, C. R., & Minton, L. (2011). *Uncovering student thinking in mathematics, grades K–5: 25 formative assessment probes for the elementary classroom.* Thousand Oaks, CA: Corwin.

Wiliam, D. (2011). *Embedded formative assessment.* Bloomington, IN: Solution Tree.

Wiliam, D., & Leahy, S. (2015). *Embedding formative assessment: Practical techniques for K–12 classrooms.* West Palm Beach, FL: Learning Sciences International.

Wiliam, D. T., & Thompson, M. (2006). Integrating assessment with learning: What will it take to make it work? In C. A. Dwyer (Ed.), *The future of assessment: Shaping, teaching, and learning* (pp. 53–82). Mahwah, NJ: Erlbaum.

Wylie, E. C., Gullickson, A., Cummings, K., Egelson, P., Noakes, L., Norman, K., & Veeder, S. (2012). *Improving formative assessment practice to empower student learning.* Thousand Oaks, CA: Corwin.

Index

Addition:
  decimal addition, 21
  partial sum, 22
Algebra:
  linear equations, 18
  linear modeling, 21
  multiplying polynomials, 19
  number sentences, 19
  order of operations, 20
  quadratic equations, 19
  rate of change, 21
  See also Expressions/equations;
      Operations/algebraic thinking
Area, 18, 20
  surface area, 20
  triangles, 19, 21
Arline, C., 36, 44, 59, 90, 101, 158, 160, 173, 177,
  180, 216
Assessment as learning, 2
Assessment for learning, 2, 5

Bar graphs, 22

Claim Cards strategy, 5
Cohen, E., 104
Comment Coding strategy, 31
  caveats with, 34
  codes for, 32–33
  cross-discipline use of, 34
  data analysis, 18
  description of, 31
  design/administration of, 32–33
  implementation attributes for, 33
  instructional decisions and, 31–32
  mathematical practices and, 23
  mathematics standards and, 33
  modifications of, 33
  student learning, promotion of, 31
Common Core State Standards (CCSS), 4
Common Core State Standards for Mathematics
  (CCSSO), 15, 16, 149
Concept Mix-Up Probes strategy, 35
  algebraic expressions, 18, 35, 36 (figure)
  caveats with, 37
  cross-discipline use of, 37
  description of, 35
  design/administration of, 35–36
  implementation attributes of, 37
  instructional decisions and, 35
  mathematical practices and, 23
  mathematics standards and, 36

  modifications of, 37
  student learning, promotion of, 35
Confidence Level Assessment (CLA)
    strategy, 17, 38
  array model of multiplication, 18
  caveats with, 40
  cross-discipline use of, 40
  description of, 38
  design/administration of, 39, 39 (figure)
  implementation attributes of, 40
  instructional decisions and, 38–39
  mathematical practices and, 23
  mathematics standards and, 40
  modifications of, 40
  student learning, promotion of, 38
Conjecture Cards strategy, 41
  caveats with, 43
  cross-discipline use of, 43
  description of, 41
  design/administration of, 41–43, 42 (figure)
  implementation attributes of, 43
  inequalities and, 18, 43, 44 (figure)
  instructional decisions and, 41
  mathematical practices and, 23
  mathematics standards and, 43
  modifications of, 43
  student learning, promotion of, 41
Correlation, 21
Counting/cardinality:
  tens, 21
  See also Number/quantity; Number system
Cover-Up strategy, 46
  caveats with, 48
  cross-discipline use of, 49
  description of, 46
  design/administration of, 46–48
  equivalent fractions, 18
  implementation attributes of, 48
  instructional decisions and, 46
  mathematical practices and, 23
  mathematics standards and, 48
  modifications of, 48
  student learning, promotion of, 46
Creighton, S. J., 125, 188, 200

Data. *See* Measurement/data
de Bono, E., 149
Decimals, 20
  comparing decimals, 22
  decimal addition, 21
Distributive property, 21, 22

231

A SAGE Publishing Company

Helping educators make the greatest impact

CORWIN HAS ONE MISSION: to enhance education through intentional professional learning.

We build long-term relationships with our authors, educators, clients, and associations who partner with us to develop and continuously improve the best evidence-based practices that establish and support lifelong learning.

The National Council of Teachers of Mathematics is the public voice of mathematics education, supporting teachers to ensure equitable mathematics learning of the highest quality for all students through vision, leadership, professional development, and research.

Why Corwin Mathematics?

We've all heard this—"either you are a math person, or you are not." At Corwin Mathematics, we believe ALL students should have the opportunity to be successful in math! Trusted experts in math education such as Linda Gojak, Ruth Harbin Miles, John SanGiovanni, Skip Fennell, Gary Martin, and many more offer clear and practical guidance to help all students move from surface to deep mathematical understanding, from favoring procedural knowledge over conceptual learning, and from rote memorization to true comprehension. **We deliver research-based, high-quality content that is classroom-tested and ready to be used in your lessons**—today!

Through books, videos, consulting, and online tools, we offer a truly **blended learning experience that helps teachers demystify math for students.** The user-friendly design and format of our resources provides not only the best classroom-based professional guidance, but many activities, lesson plans, rubrics, and templates to help you implement changes at your own pace in order to sustain learning improvement over time. We are **committed to empowering every learner.** With our forward-thinking and practical offerings, Corwin Mathematics helps you enable all students to realize the power and beauty of math and its connection to everything they do.

Warm Regards,
The Corwin Mathematics Team

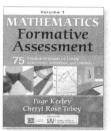

CPSIA information can be obtained
at www.ICGtesting.com
Printed in the USA
LVHW102245050919
630139LV00011B/787/P